S'nim Oh
Wishes

KERBER
EDITION YOUNG ART

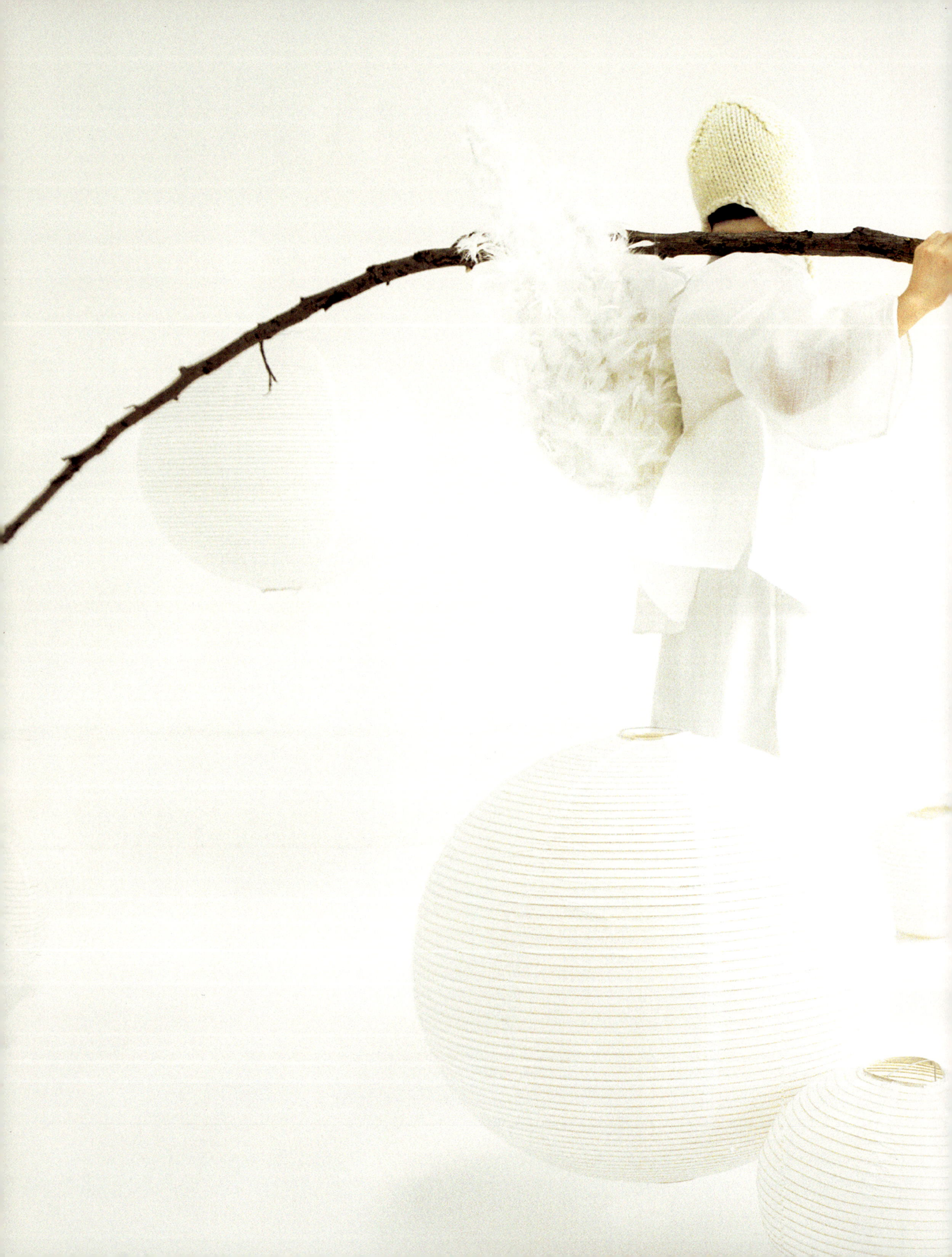

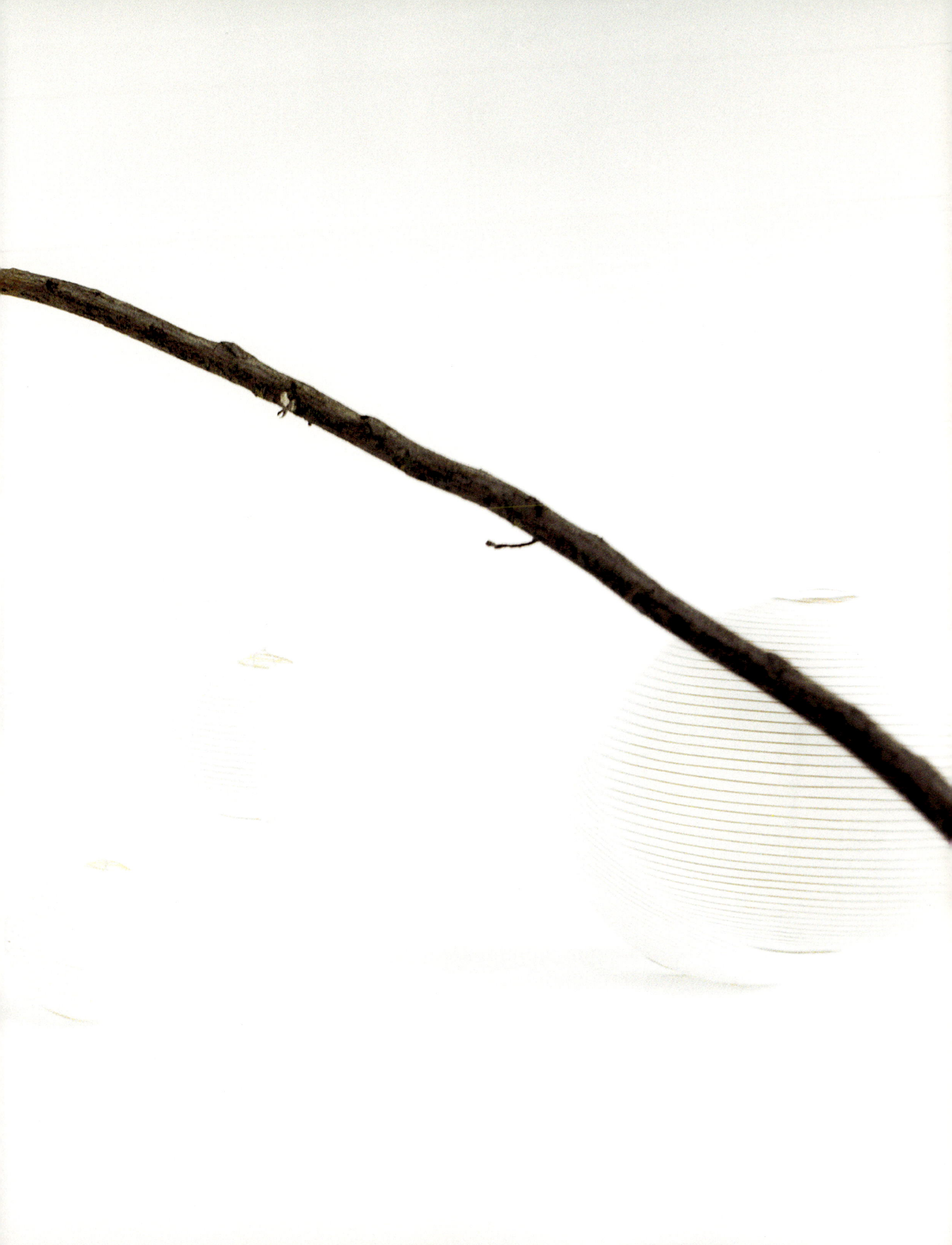

Inhalt / Content

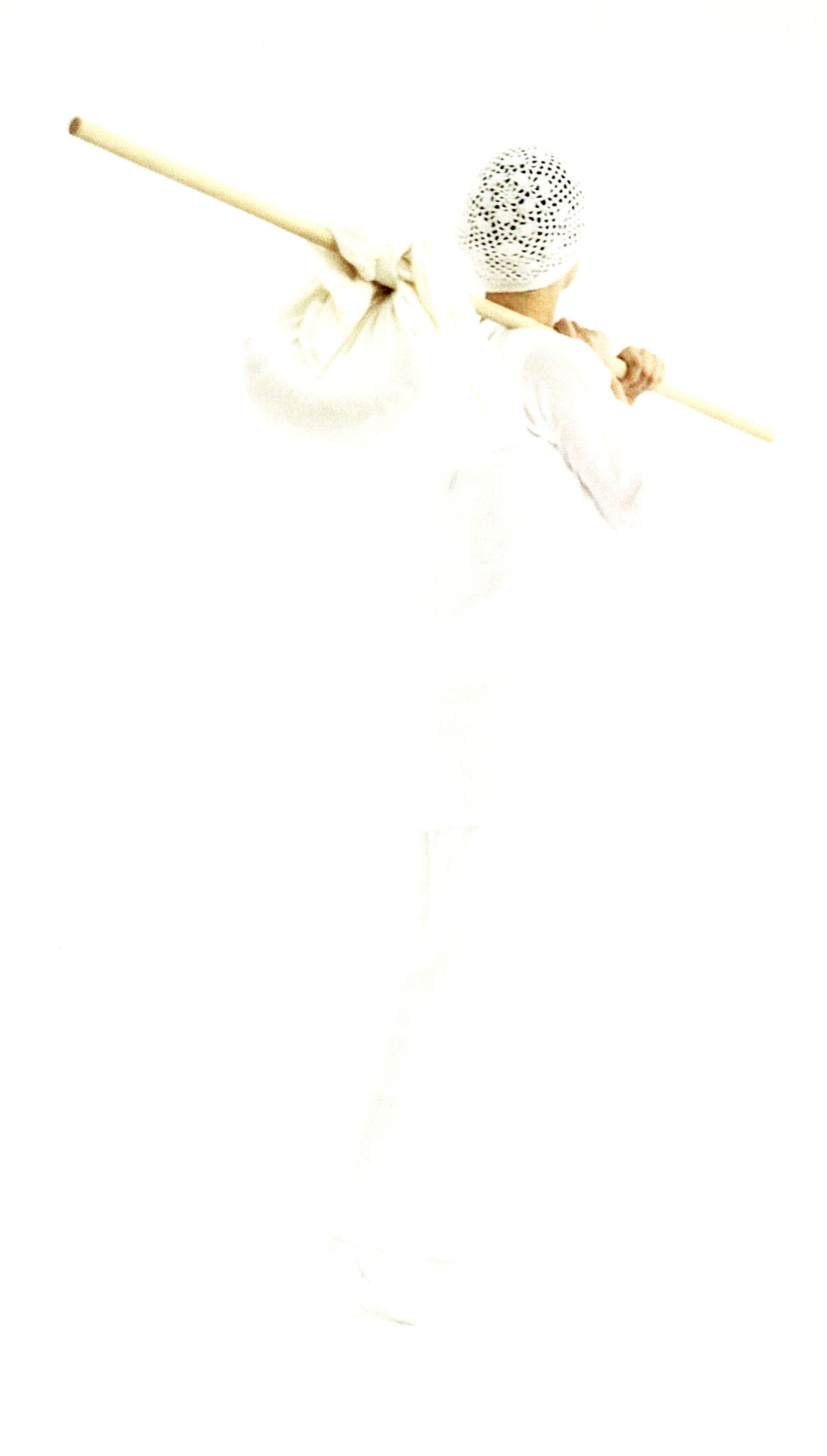

Wishes

Annette Doms

Wünsche bedeuten ein HYPERLINK »http://de.wikipedia.org/wiki/Mensch« menschliches HYPERLINK »http://de.wikipedia.org/wiki/Gef%C3%BChl« Gefühl oder ein menschlicher HYPERLINK »http://de.wikipedia.org/wiki/Gedanke« Gedanke, der eine Veränderung der HYPERLINK »http://de.wikipedia.org/wiki/Realit%C3%A4t«Realität herbei sehnt. Sehr oft sind sie Fiktionen, die anders erfüllt werden, als es sich der Wünschende erhofft. Nicht selten haben sie magischen Charakter. Das Ausmaß der unerfüllten Wünsche bleibt ungezählt. Im Märchen hat der Protagonist meist drei Wünsche frei. Was denkt sich die Philosophin S'nim Oh, wenn sie einem Großteil ihrer Werke den Titel »wishes« gibt? Ist es der Wunsch nach Muse und Ruhe, der in ihren Bildern deutlich zum Ausdruck kommt? Oder ist es der Wunsch sich selbst als Mensch zu formen, nimmt doch die Selbstinszenierung einen weiten Spielraum im Schaffensprozess der Künstlerin ein.

Bekannt ist S'nim Oh vor allem für ihre Fotoserien, in denen der konzeptionelle Ansatz der Künstlerin deutlich zum Ausdruck kommt. Konstante Themen sind die Auseinandersetzung mit den Nichtigkeiten des Daseins und der Philosophie des Geistes. Die Serie »wishes« zieht sich dabei wie ein roter Faden durch das Werk der Künstlerin, die stets in Form von fotografischen Selbstporträts in verschiedenen Kostümierungen auftritt.

Leise steht oder bewegt sie sich in ihren selbst gestalteten Bühnenbildern, die von den aufwendigen, mit Kunstlicht beleuchteten Studioaufnahmen ablenken. An, auf und neben S'nim Oh tauchen Requisiten auf, derer sie sich aus dem Alltag bedient, dekontextualisiert und zum ästhetischen Kunstobjekt macht. Sie verwendet gelbe Putzlappen oder rosafarbene Servietten, die zusammengenäht ein fein anmutendes Gewand ergeben und spielt dabei subtil mit der sozialen Stellung der Frau. Sie steht in leicht gekippter Haltung und traditioneller Tracht gekleidet auf einem Haufen Reiskörner, währenddessen ein anderes Bild sie in gleicher Tracht auf einem Berg von geschrederten Geldscheinen zeigt. Die Pose hat sich verändert, die schräge Haltung mit dem herabhängenden Gewand ist nun kerzengerade und selbstsicher, das Kleid ist inzwischen geschlossenen und fest zugeschnürt. Der sensible Blick der Künstlerin spielt dabei mit Symbolen der westlichen Überflussgesellschaft, indem sie Gegenwelten schafft und das Alltägliche der Dinge zu überwinden versucht. Ein großer Gewinn ihrer Arbeiten besteht in der Schulung des Auges und des Denkens, denn sowohl in der visuellen als auch in der inhaltlichen Ausführung werden strenge Anforderungen an den Betrachter gestellt. So zum Beispiel in einer Reihe von Fotografien, in denen die Künstlerin in einem bunten, mit Blumen verzierten Sommerkleid und Pelzmütze auftritt. Die konträre Kombination der Kleiderwahl wird durch einen Gürtel aus weißen Luftballons in Birnenform ergänzt. Die Reihung dieses Motivs, indem die Künstlerin steht, kniet oder sitzt, suggeriert Bewegung und stellt die Frage nach dem Sinn des Spiels mit dem Luftballon. Der Luftballon ist ein mit Luft gefüllter elastischer Hohlkörper mit geringer Haltbarkeit. S'nim Oh verwendet ihn hier als Dekorationsgegenstand, der ihren Körper schmückt. Im Bewusstsein, dass der Luftballon wie eine Seifenblase jederzeit zerplatzen kann, dient er ihr aber auch als Vanitas-Symbol, das in moralisierender Absicht an die Vergänglichkeit des Lebens, die Kindheit und die irdischen Materialien erinnert.

S'nim Oh baut Welten auf, in denen sich Wünsche und Sehnsüchte breit machen. Jedes Bild zeigt eine andere S'nim Oh. Mal blickt sie Gedanken verloren, mal konzentriert, zeigt sie sich von der Seite oder versteckt sich hinter ihrem »Arbeitsmaterial«. Manche dieser Bilder wirken wie Momentaufnahmen, in denen die Künstlerin zur Pose erstarrt. Dass dahinter viele Stunden und manchmal mehrere Tage Arbeit stecken, sieht man ihnen nicht mehr an. S'nim Oh ist bemüht um die Verwirklichung eines Ideals, das sich der kritisch-rationalen Selbstüberprüfung ihres Denkens unterzieht. Zweifelsohne entwickelt sie dabei eine eigene Sicht der Dinge, die das scheinbar Zweifelsfreie und Selbstverständliche in Frage stellen. Entsprechend der Definition des Wunsches zeigen S'nim Oh's Fotografien jedenfalls kein Abbild der sichtbaren Realität, als viel mehr das ihrer persönlichen, inneren Wirklichkeit. Nicht selten werden Kindheitserinnerungen der in Südkorea aufgewachsenen Künstlerin wach und werden Gedanken mit verwandten Seelen reflektiert. Ein Video der Serie »whishes«, in dem sich S'nim Oh, kniend und im buddhistischen Gewand, dem konzentrierten Werfen und Fangen von Kieselsteinen vertieft, ist Teil einer persönlichen Erinnerung der Künstlerin an koreanische Kinder, die sich mit dem Spiel der Steine ihre Zeit vertreiben. Die Steine werden in die Luft geworfen, mit dem Handrücken gefangen und auf einen immer größer werdenden Haufen gelegt. Hinter jedem geworfenen Stein verbirgt sich ein Wunsch, der bei erfolgreichem Fangen in Erfüllung gehen soll. S'nim Ohs Spiel wirkt konzentriert und angespannt, der begleitende Ton der aufeinander klackenden Steine klingt wie das fallende Wasser einer Tropfsteinhöhle. Durch die Wahl der Zeitlupe wird das Video durch Ruhe bestimmt und versetzt den Betrachter in einen kontemplativen, tranceartigen Zustand, der von der westlichen Hektik ablenkt.

Neben Fotografien und Videos schafft S'nim Oh kindlich-naive Skulpturen, die sich bewusst einer eindeutigen und sinnstifenden Interpretation entziehen. Häschen wuchern aus Galeriewänden, Lotusblüten erfüllen den Raum, Pilze werden surreal vergrößert, lachende Buddhas neben pinkfarbene Schweinchen sinnenfroh in Szene gesetzt. Der Betrachter steht davor wie vor einem Wunder, ist erstaunt, weil das vor ihm aufgebaute Bild nicht seiner assoziativen Erwartung entspricht. Vermeintlich Bekanntes ist verfremdet, herkömmliche Wahrnehmungsmuster werden sensibilisiert. Die von S'nim Oh inszenierten Erlebniswelten ergeben ein Geflecht aus Bezügen, das die Biografie der Künstlerin in mythologischen und historischen Erzählsträngen einfließen lässt. Die Kombination der sonderbaren Objekte mit Videos und Fotografien unterstreicht die Komplexität ihrer vielschichtigen Arbeiten, die eine Vielzahl von Geschichten zu erzählen scheinen, sich jedoch einer Interpretation eindeutigen entziehen.

Die Arbeiten von S'nim Oh entstehen im Spannungsfeld gesellschaftlicher Bezüge und ihrer eigenen Biografie, die stellvertretend für ihre interkulturellen Erfahrungen steht. In ihren Fotografien, Objekten und Videoprojektionen thematisiert sie diskursive Zusammenhänge aus ihrem sozialen Umfeld, ihren asiatischen Wurzeln und massenkulturellen Phänomenen der modernen Industrienationen. Nichts scheint in ihren Arbeiten den Zufall überlassen zu sein. Das Licht, die Farben und Geräusche sind aufeinander abgestimmt, die Präsentation ist exakt. S'nim Ohs Charakteristikum ist die Perfektion, die man beim Betrachten ihrer Werke deutlich spürt.

Zweifelsohne geht es S'nim Oh um die Manifestation ihrer gedanklichen Strukturen, die sie in eine ihr eigene ästhetische Bildsprache umsetzt. Zwischen den statischen Bildmotiven, den lebhaften Farben der Bilder und dem Spiel mit der Wahrnehmung besteht ein spürbares Spannungsverhältnis, das an die Sinne des Betrachters appelliert und sich zu einem tiefgründigen Selbstportrait der Künstlerin verdichtet. S'nim Oh hat in ihren Bildern eine eigene Sprache entwickelt, die durch puristische Klarheit und meditative Ruhe besticht. Ihre Fotografien, Videos und multimedialen Installationen sind Inszenierungen eines komplexen Denkens und Wirklichkeitsbezuges. Die verschiedenen Bedeutungsebenen ihrer Arbeiten erschließen sich oft erst in der Auseinadersetzung mit S'nim Ohs Herkunft und ihren traditionellen Einflüssen. Es scheint als begäbe sich S'nim Oh auf die Suche nach einer verloren Zeit ihrer Kindheit. Ihr Werk reflektiert somit eine Art Erinnerungsarbeit, die sie in die gesellschaftlichen Phänomene unserer Zeit integriert. Vergangenes wird Gegenwart, Gegenwärtiges wird zu Vergangenheit. Zeit, Raum und Rezeption stehen im Wechselspiel, werden aufgehoben und verharren im statischen Moment. Der philosophische Ansatz
in ihren Arbeiten öffnet sich jedoch mehreren Bedeutungsebenen. Man denkt an ein komplexes Labyrinth, das den Weg hindurch zum Rätsel macht. Egal wie verschlungen die Wege dabei sind. Was bleibt, ist die eindrucksvolle Ästhetik, die dem Werk von S'nim Oh eine poetische Aura verleiht.

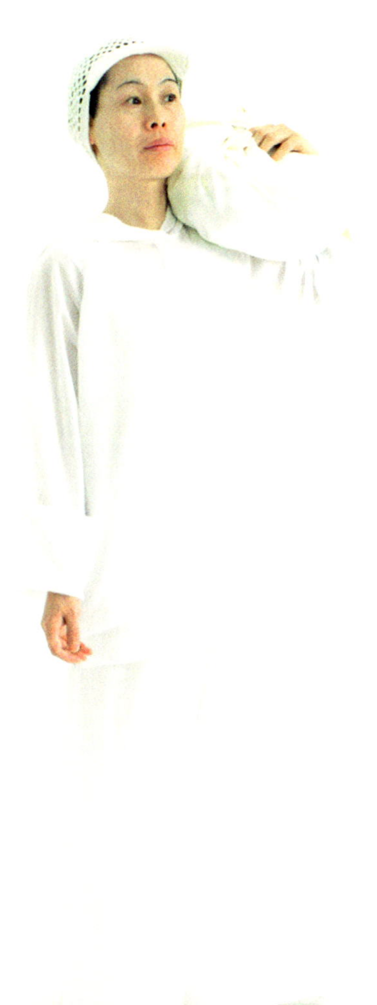

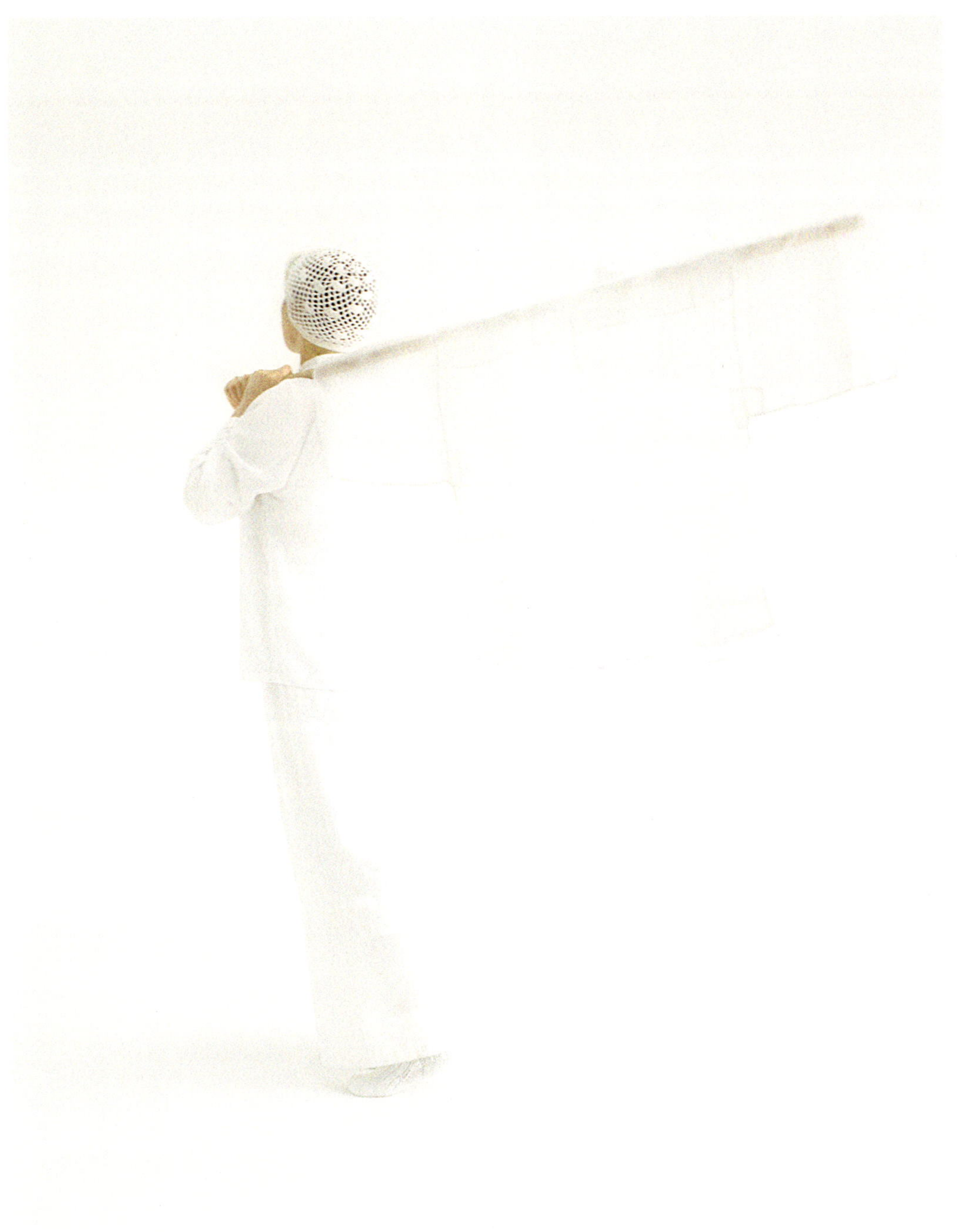

Wishes, 2005

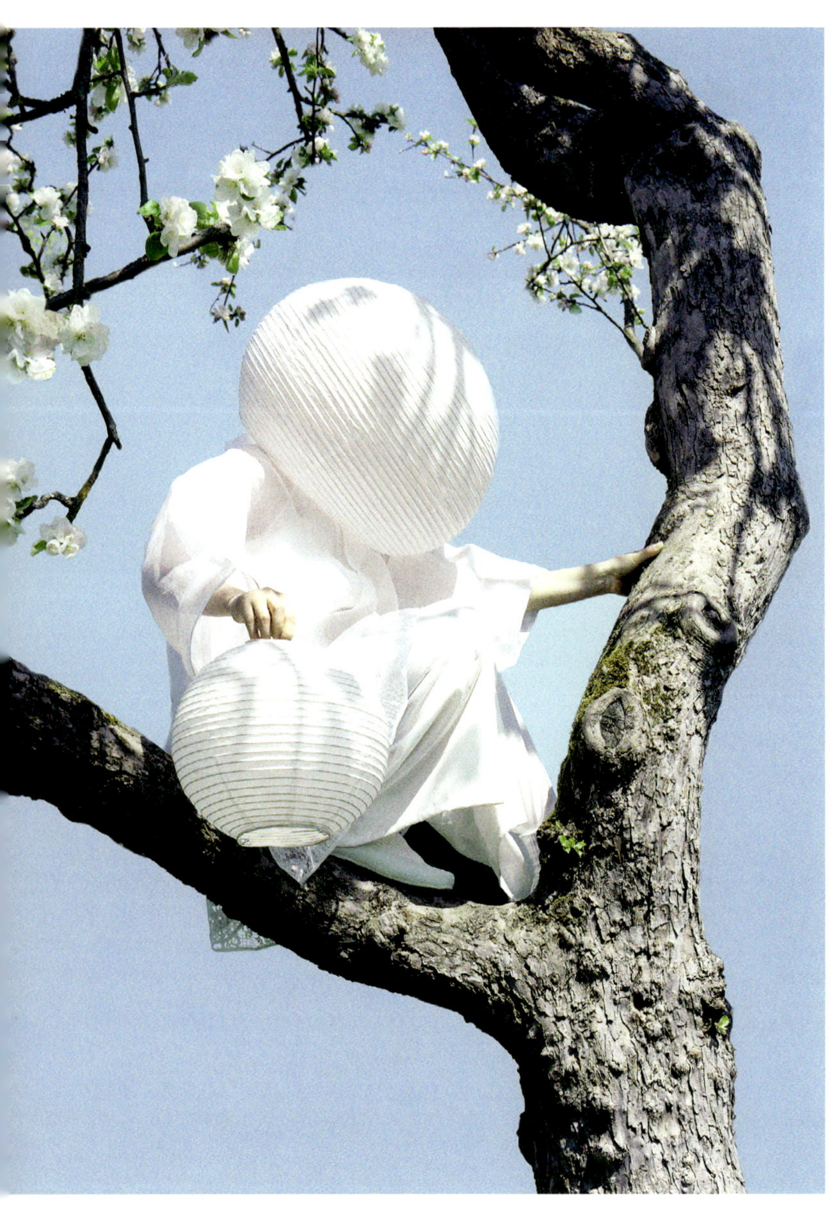

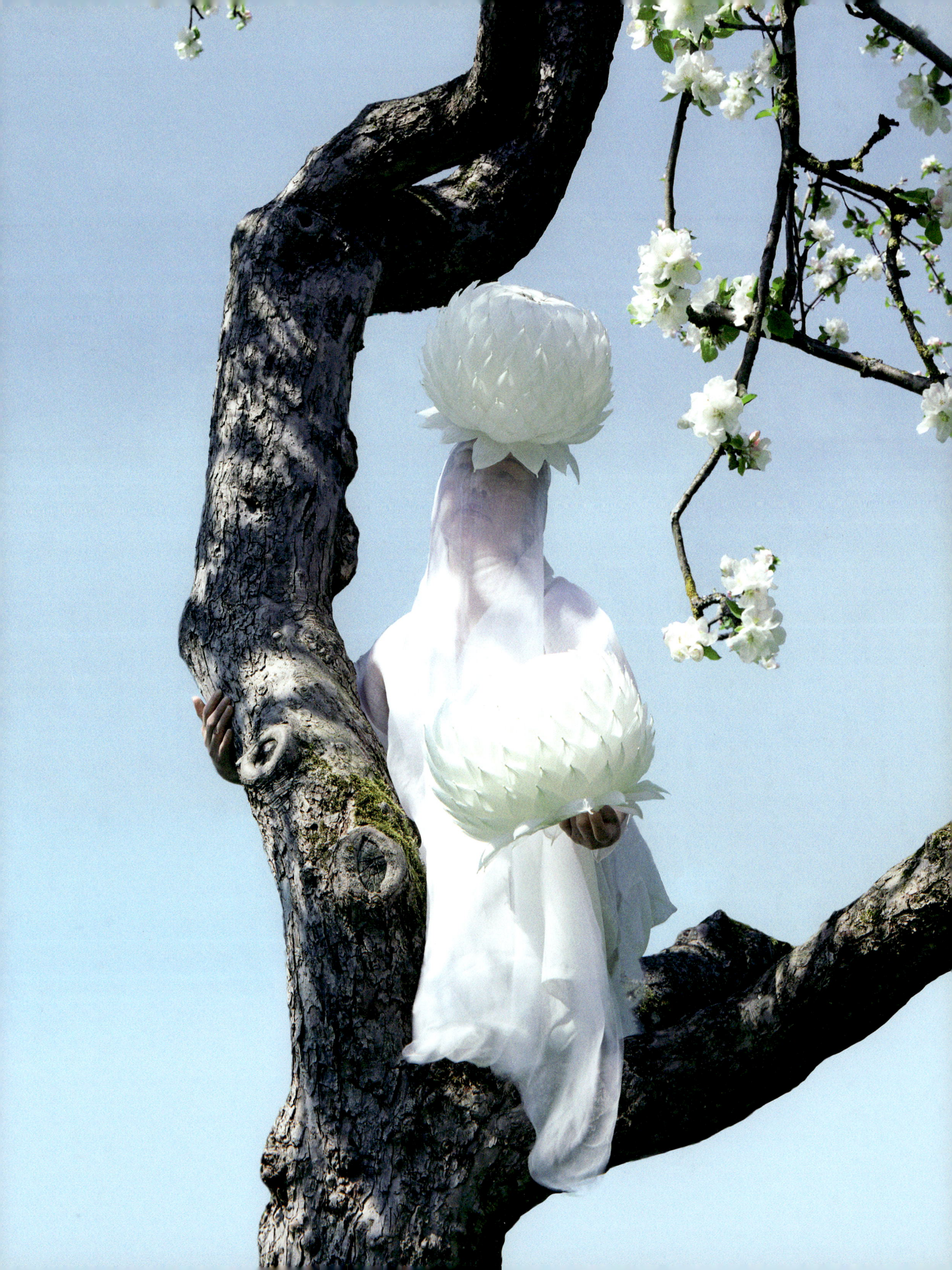

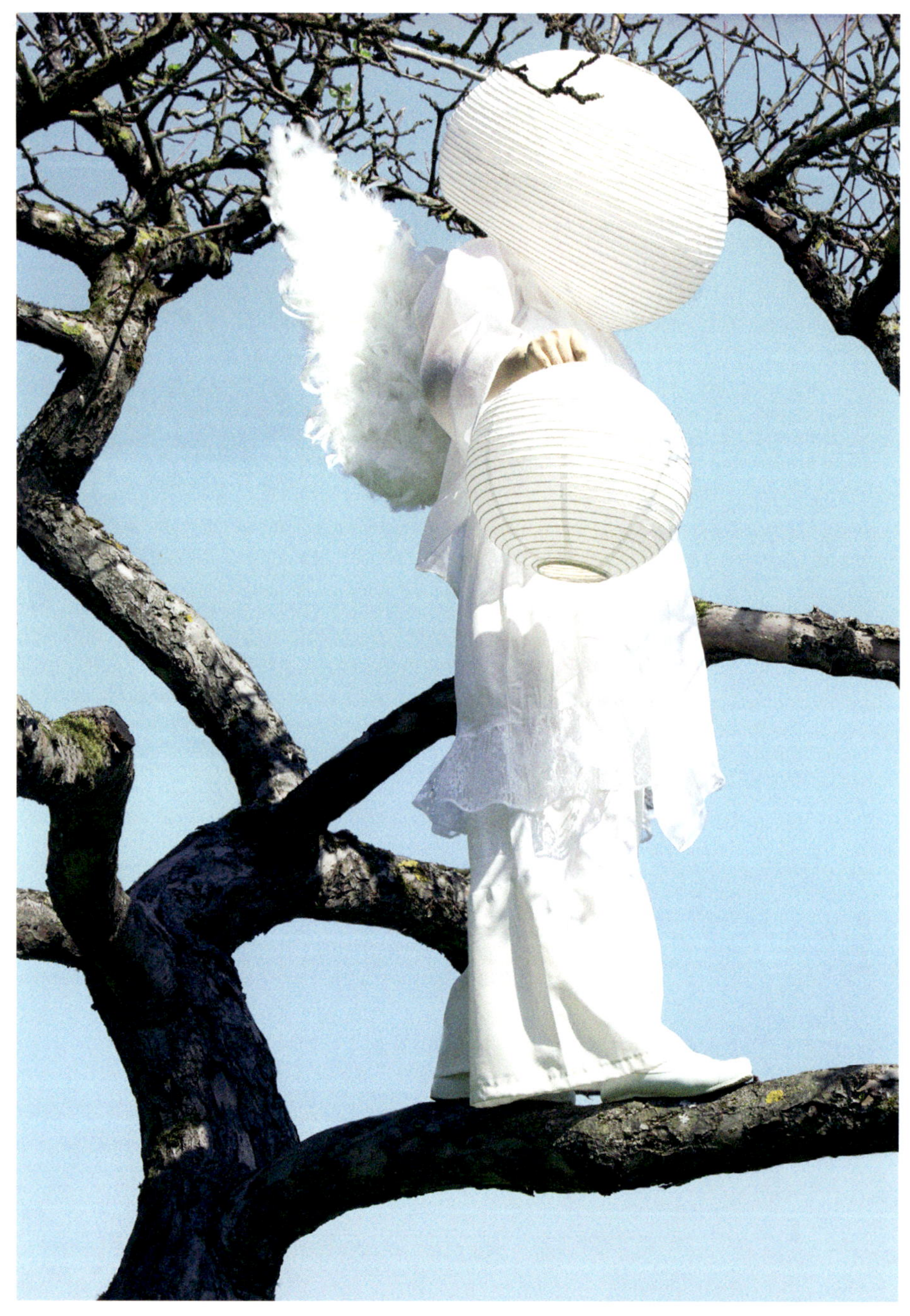

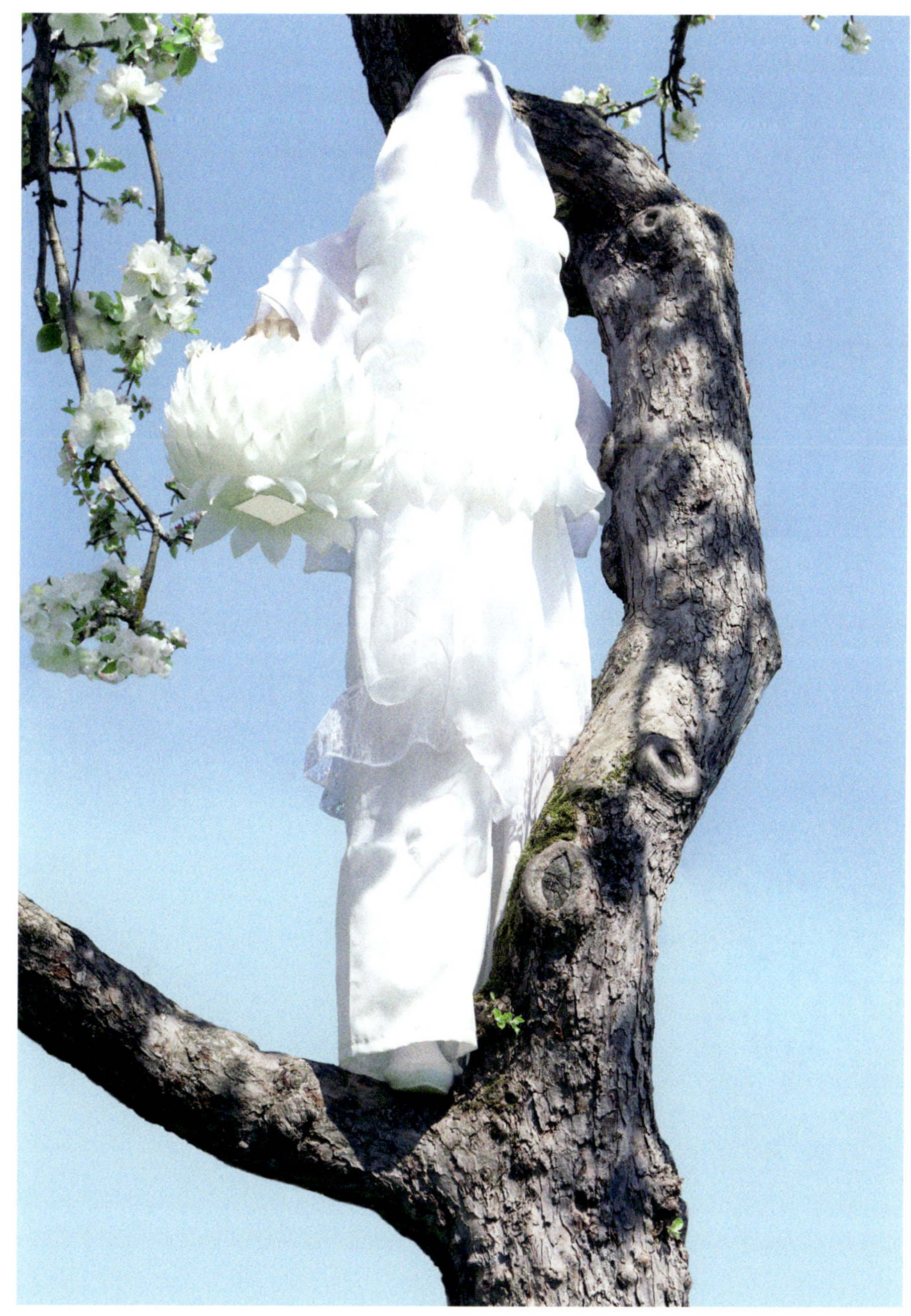

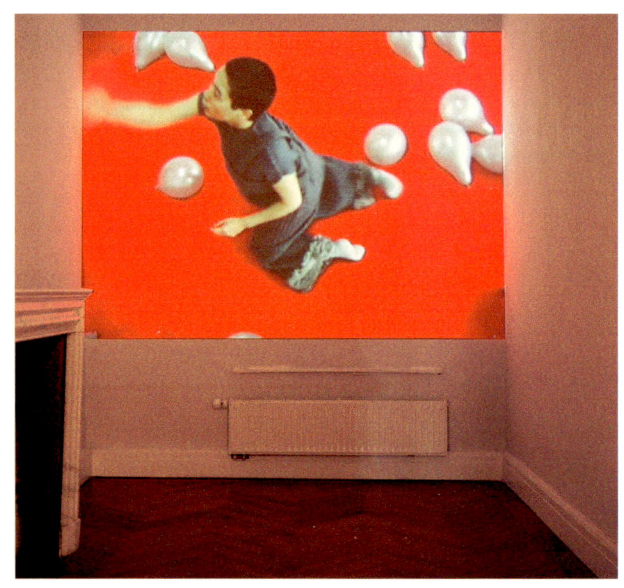

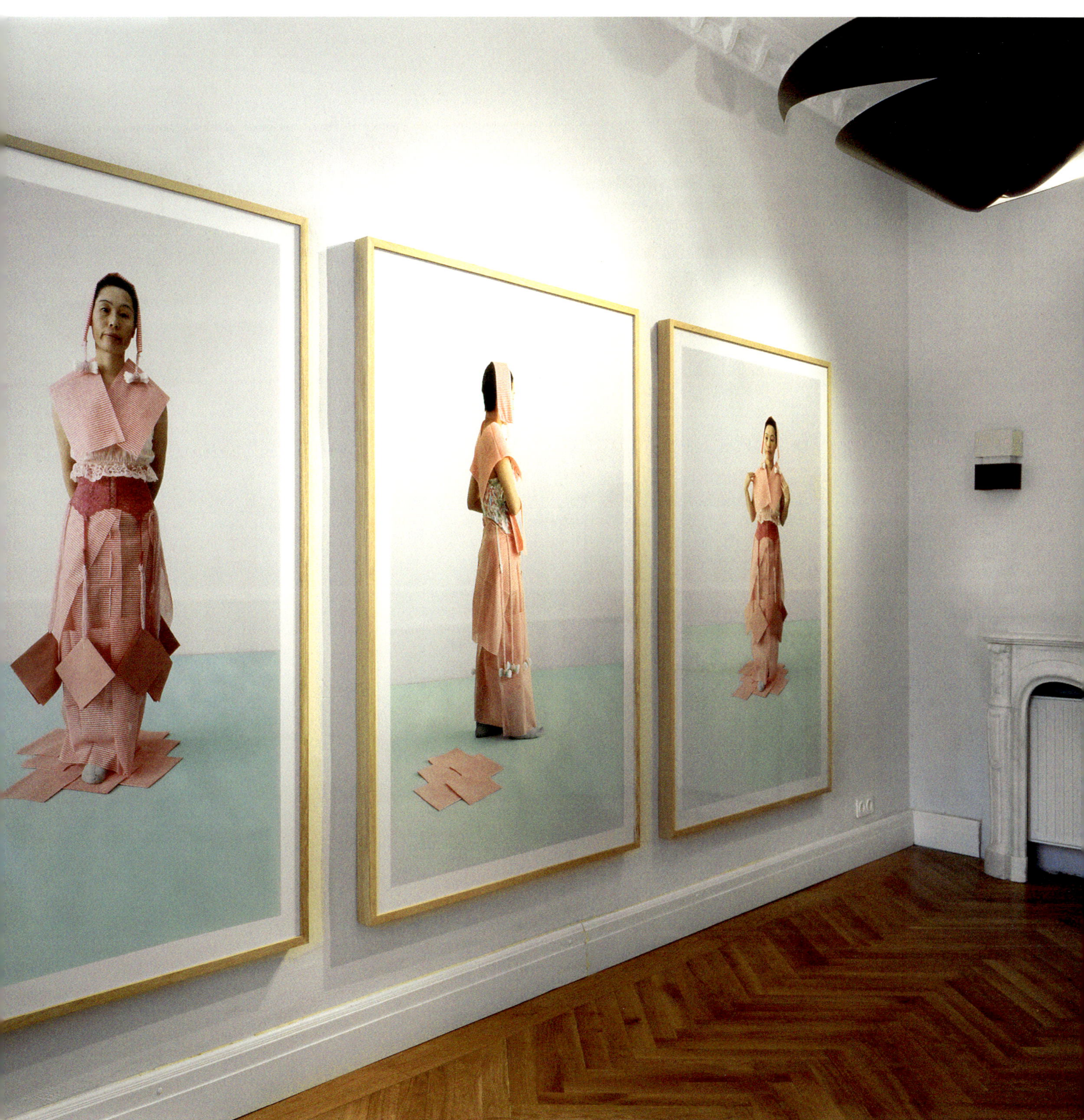

Galerie der Moderne Stefan Vogdt, 2005

Annette Doms

Wishes

The word »wishes« means a HYPERLINK »http://de.wikipedia.org/wiki/Mensch« human HYPERLINK »http://de.wikipedia.org/wiki/Gef%C3%BChl« feeling or a human HYPERLINK »http://de.wikipedia.org/wiki/Gedanke« thought that longs for a change of HYPERLINK »http://de.wikipedia.org/wiki/Realit%C3%A4t« reality. Very often they are fictions that can be fulfilled in unhoped-for ways. Frequently they have a magical character. The number of unfulfilled wishes remains uncounted. In fairy tales the protagonist is usually granted three wishes. What does philosopher S'nim Oh think when she titles many of her works wishes? Is it a desire for inspiration and quiet, which is obviously expressed in her images? Or is it the desire to shape herself as a human being – for, after all, the task of presenting the self requires a great deal of room to play within the creative process of the artist.

S'nim Oh is especially known for her series of photographs in which the artist's conceptual approach is clearly articulated. Constant themes are the exploration of the nothingness of being and the philosophy of the mind/spirit. The wishes series is a recurrent theme in the artist's work, which is always in the form of photographs of herself in diverse costumes.

Quietly she stands in or moves through the settings she herself has created, which draw attention away from the complex, artificially lit studio photographs. With, on, and next to S'nim Oh appear props taken from everyday life, decontextualized and turned into aesthetic objets d'art. She uses yellow dusting cloths or pink napkins, which, when sewn together, give the appearance of a delicate gown and thus subtly play with women's social position. She stands, slightly leaning to one side, dressed in a traditional costume, on a pile of rice, while in another image she is wearing the same costume and stands on a mountain of shredded currency. The pose has altered: the tilted posture with the drooping gown is now as straight as a post and self-confident; the dress has been closed and tightly fastened. The artist's sensitive view plays with symbols drawn from the western society of excess, employing attempts to create counter-worlds and overcome the ordinariness of things. One great benefit of her works is in the way they educate the eye and mind, for the execution of the work makes rigorous demands of the viewer in terms of both the visual as well as the contextual information – for instance, in a series of photographs in which the artist appears in a colorful, flowery summer dress and fur cap. A pear-shaped belt made of white balloons supplements the contradictory combination of clothing. The order of this series – in which the artist stands, kneels, or sits – suggests motion and asks the reason for playing with balloons. The balloon is an empty mass filled with air whose existence will be short-lived. S'nim Oh uses it here as a decorative object to ornament her body. Conscious that the balloon could burst at any

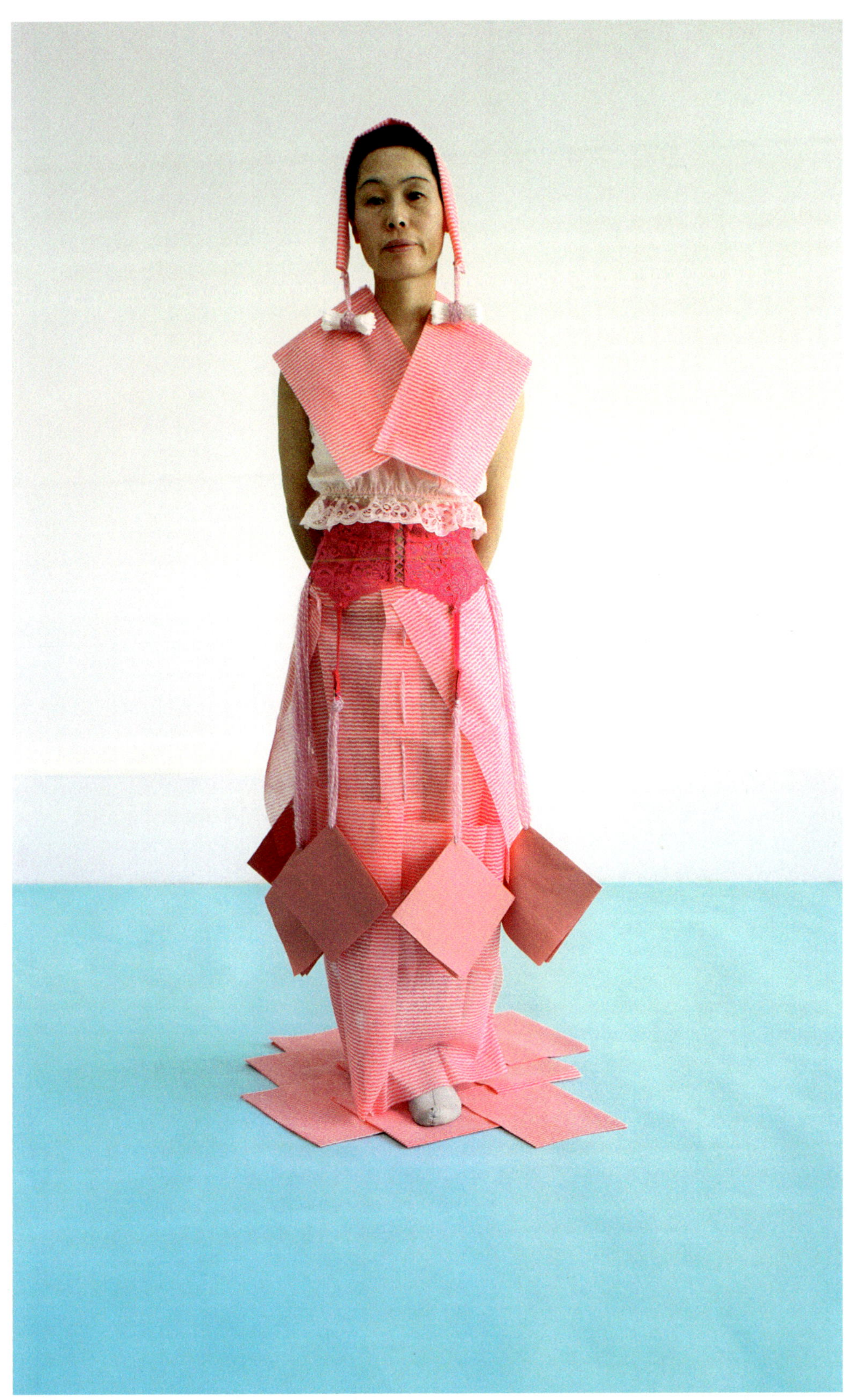

Wishes, 2005

time, like a soap bubble, it also serves as a vanitas symbol that recalls, with moral intent, the temporality of life, childhood, and all things Earthly.

S'nim Oh constructs worlds in which wishes and longings are widespread. Each picture shows a different S'nim Oh. Sometimes she seems lost in thought, sometimes in concentration; sometimes she is seen from the side or hidden behind her »work material.« Some of these photographs seem like snapshots in which the artist is frozen in the pose. The many hours and sometimes days of work behind them can no longer be seen. S'nim Oh is attempting to realize an ideal that is subjected to the critical, rational scrutiny of her thoughts. Doubtless in doing so she develops her own view of things, which questions matters that are considered indubitable or matter-of- course. In accordance with the definition of the wish, S'nim Oh's photographs do not show the reproduction of visible reality, but rather, her personal, internal reality. Often memories of her childhood in South Korea are awakened and thoughts of related souls are reflected. A video from the wishes series features S'nim Oh, kneeling and wearing a Buddhist robe. She is absorbed in a concentrated game of throwing and catching pebbles, one of the artist's personal memories of how Korean children spend their time playing this game with stones. Pebbles are thrown into the air, caught on the back of the hand, and added to an increasingly large pile. Behind each stone is concealed a wish, which is supposed to be fulfilled if the stone is caught. S'nim Oh's game seems concentrated and tense; the noise of clashing stones sounds like water dripping in a stalagmite cave. Since the video is played in a loop, it is determined by a sense of calm and puts the viewer into a contemplative, trance-like state that distracts from the hectic activities of the west.

Besides photographs and videos, S'nim Oh makes childlike, naive sculptures that consciously avoid clear, reasonable interpretation. Bunnies grow into gallery walls, lotus flowers fill the space, mushrooms are surrealistically enlarged; laughing, joyful Buddhas are positioned next to pink pigs in the scene. The viewer stands before all of this as if witnessing a miracle, is astonished because the image constructed in front of him does not conform to his expectations. Familiar things seem strange, usual patterns of perception are sensitized. S'nim Oh's experiential worlds interweave to create a fabric of references that includes mythological and historical threads of the artist's biography. Combining strange objects with videos and photographs underscores the complexity of her multilayered works, which seem to tell a number of stories, but at the same time, cannot be clearly interpreted.

S'nim Oh's works are created in the intriguing environment of social relations and her own biography, which represents her intercultural experiences. In her photographs, objects, and videos, her theme has to do with discursive contexts from the society surrounding, her Asian roots, and the modern mass culture phenomena found in industrialized nations. Nothing in her works seems left to chance. The light, the colors, and the noises go together, the presentation is exact. Perfection is characteristic of S'nim Oh, and it is clearly felt when viewing her work.

Without a doubt, S'nim Oh is concerned with the manifestation of her conceptual structures, which she transposes into her own aesthetic visual language. Among the static visual motifs, the vivid colors of the images, and the way they play with perception is a palpably tense relationship that appeals to the viewer's reason, condensing to become a profound self-portrait of the artist. In her photographs, S'nim Oh has developed her own vernacular whose purist clarity and meditative calm is enchanting. Her photographs, videos, and multimedia installations are presentations of complex thought and references to reality. Frequently, the different levels of meaning in her works can only be comprehended through the exploration of her heritage and traditional influences. It seems as if S'nim Oh is on a quest to find a lost time of her childhood. Her work thus reflects a kind of mnemonic task, which she integrates into the social phenomena of our time. The past becomes the present; what is present becomes past. Time, space, and reception interweave, disappear, and are frozen in stasis. The philosophical approach to her works, however, opens up several levels of meaning. We are reminded of a complex labyrinth that turns the path through it into a riddle. Regardless of how twisted the paths are. What remains is the impressive aesthetic, which lends S'nim Oh's work a poetic aura.

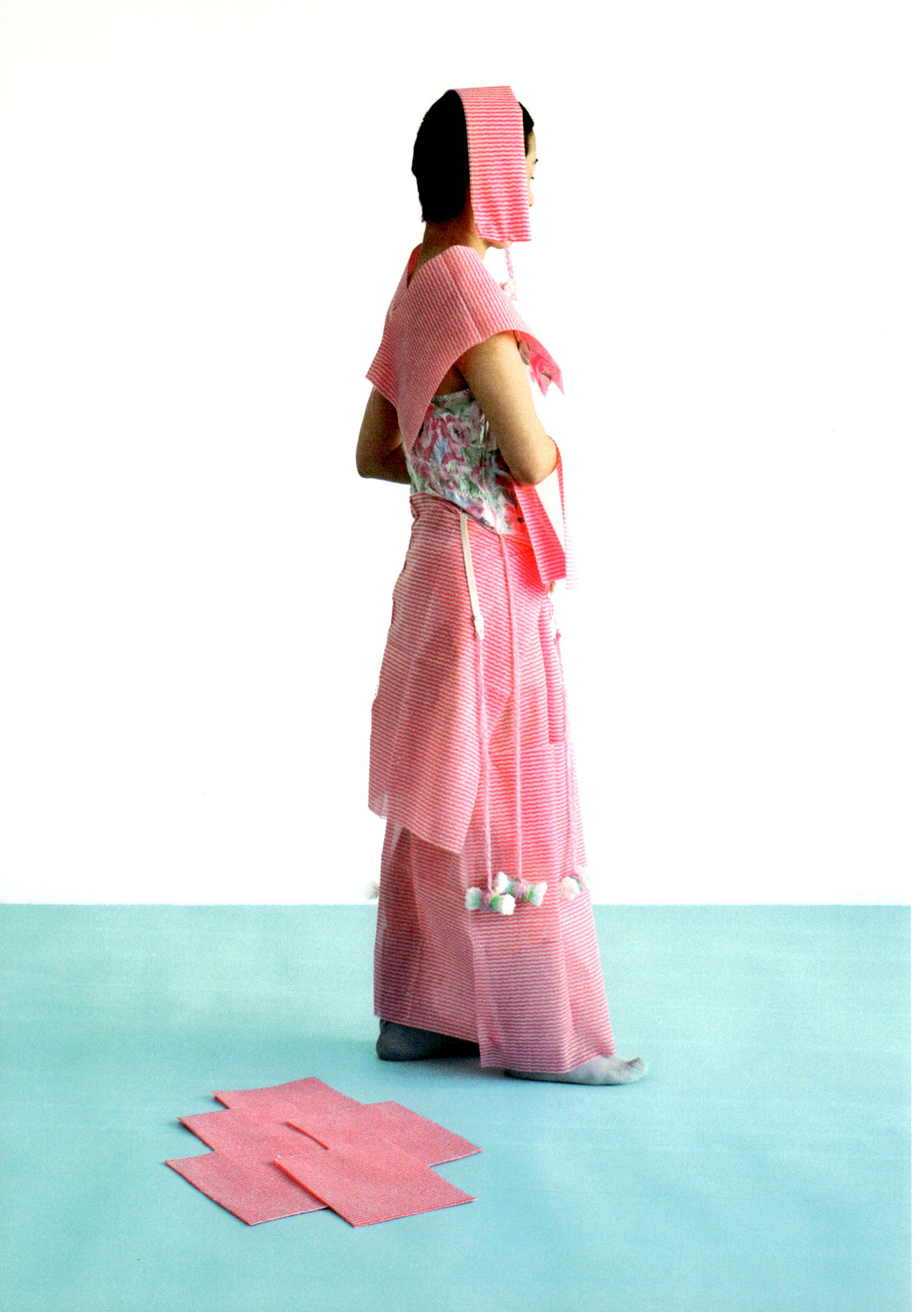

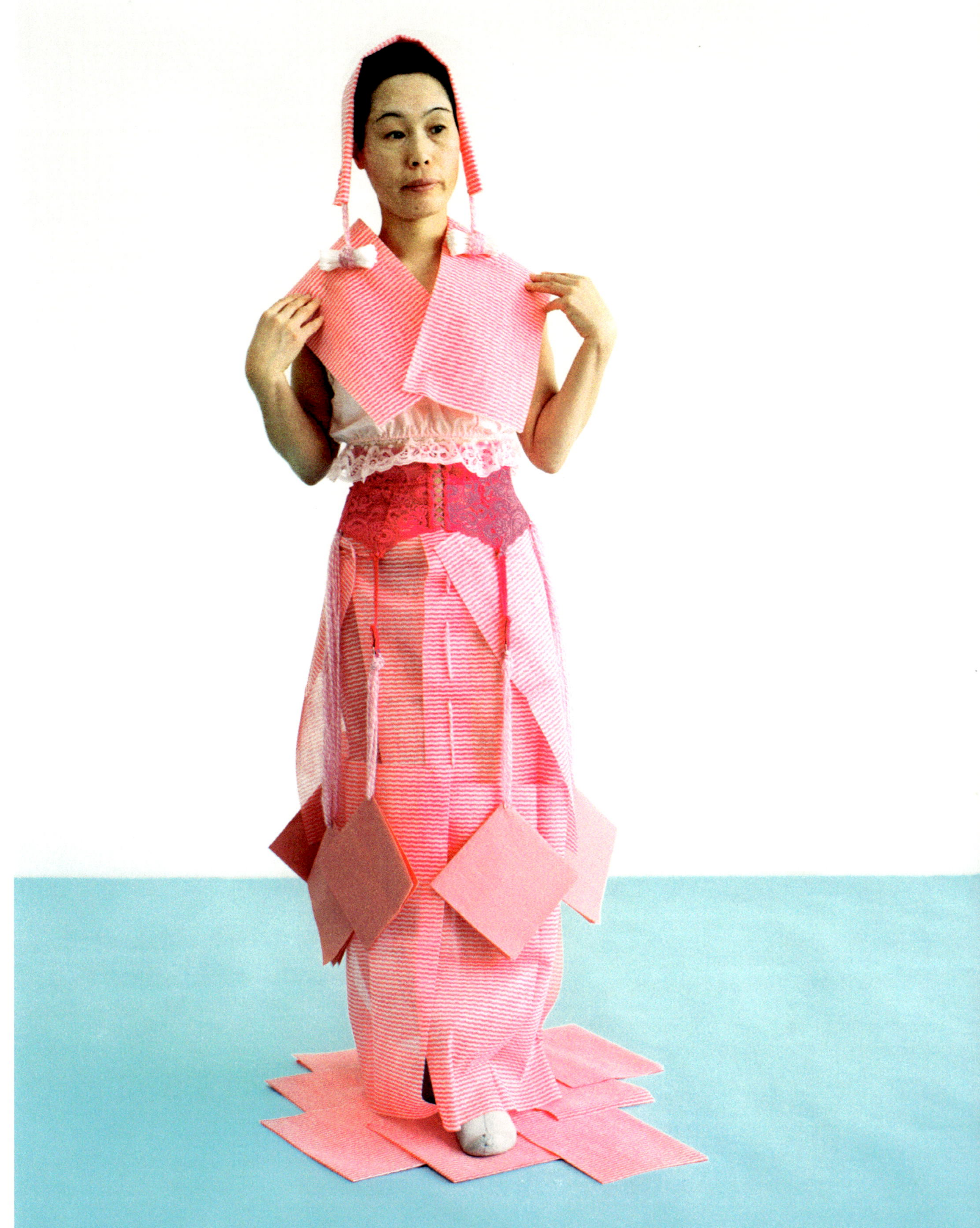

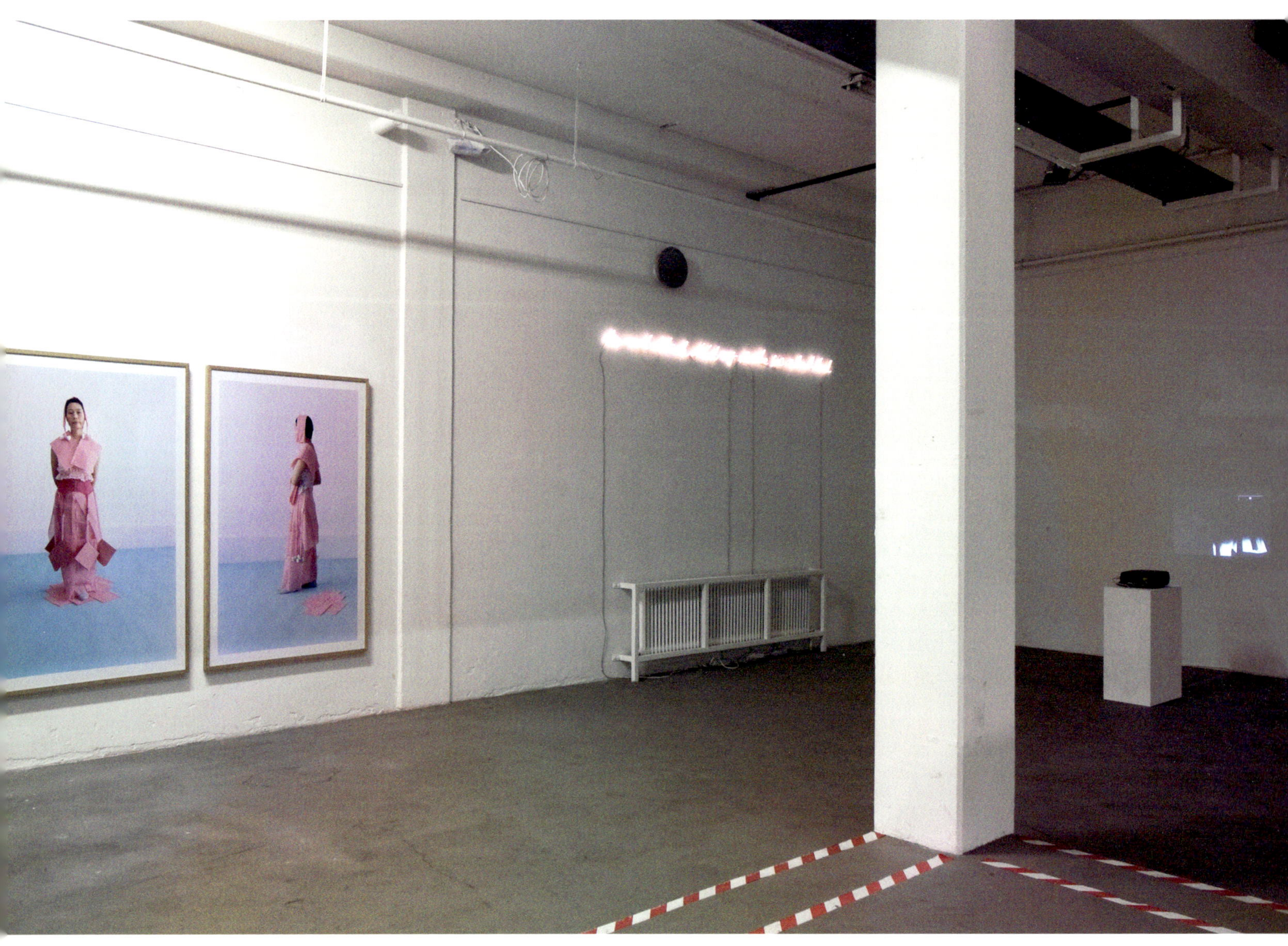

White Box, München 2005

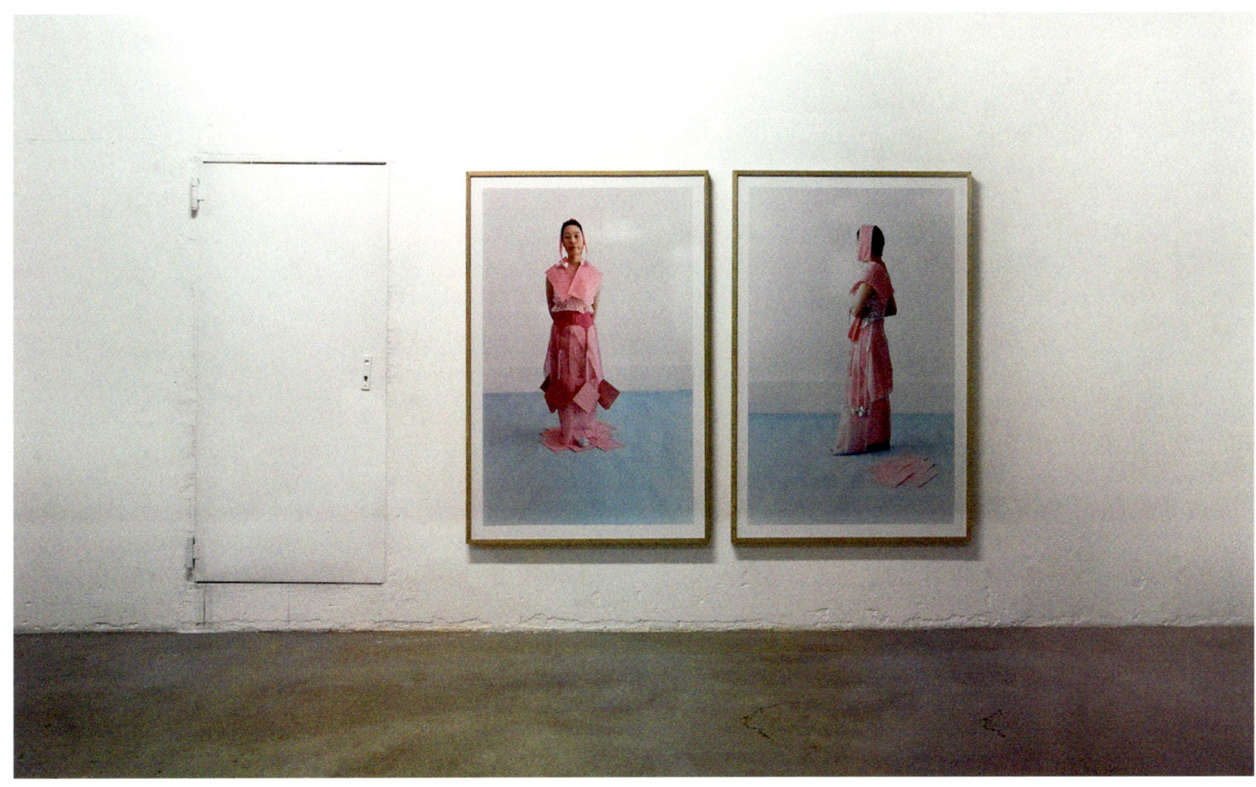

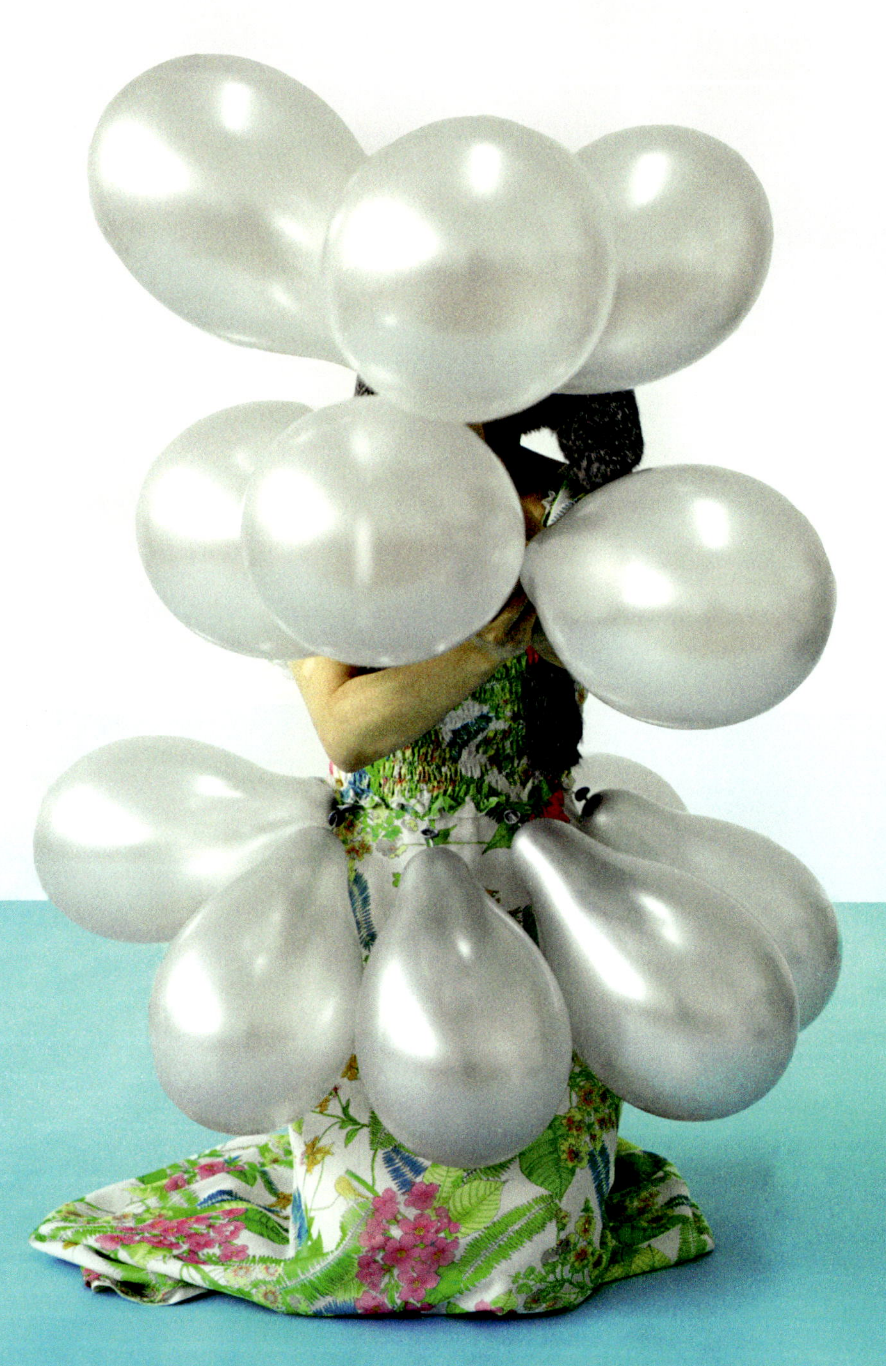

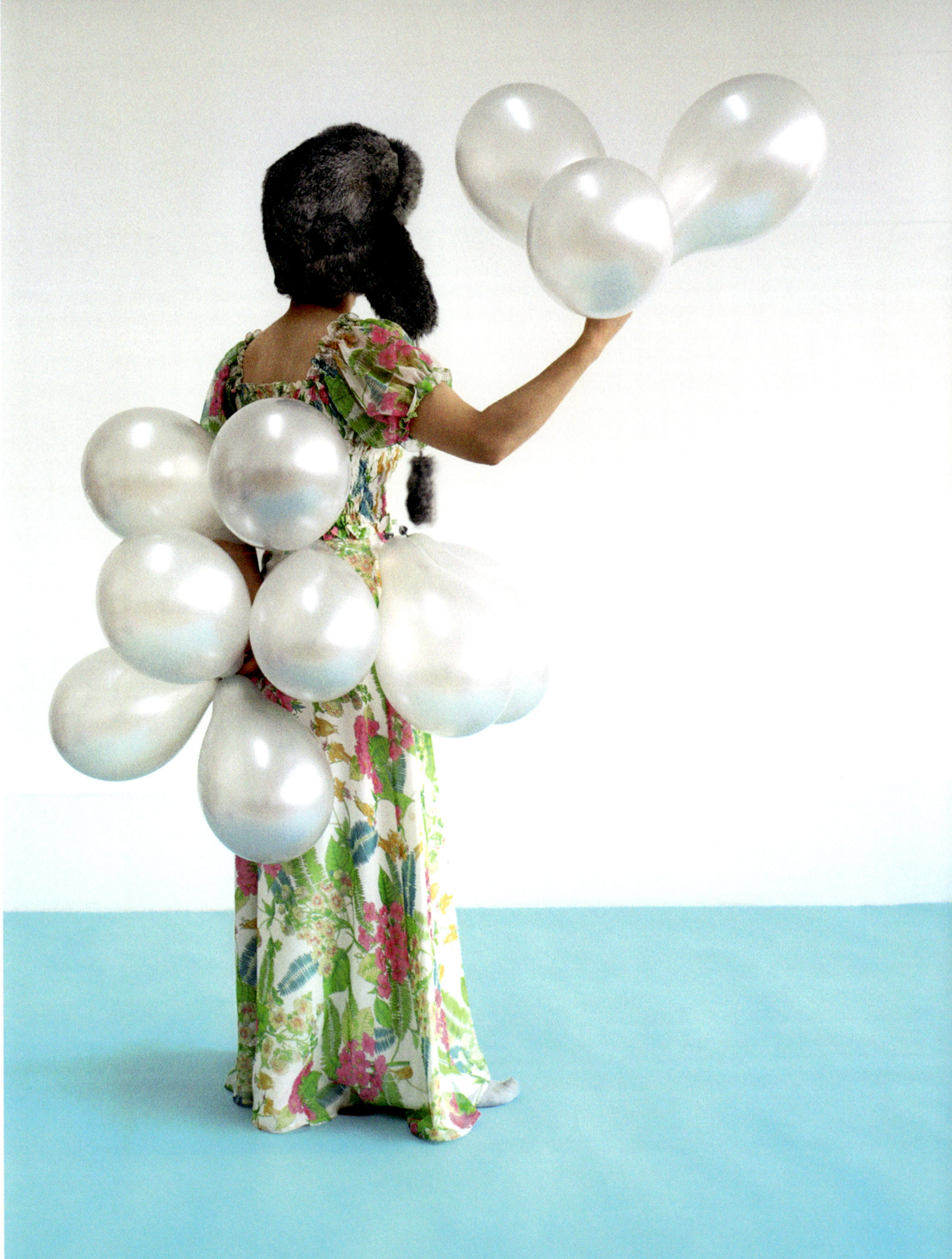

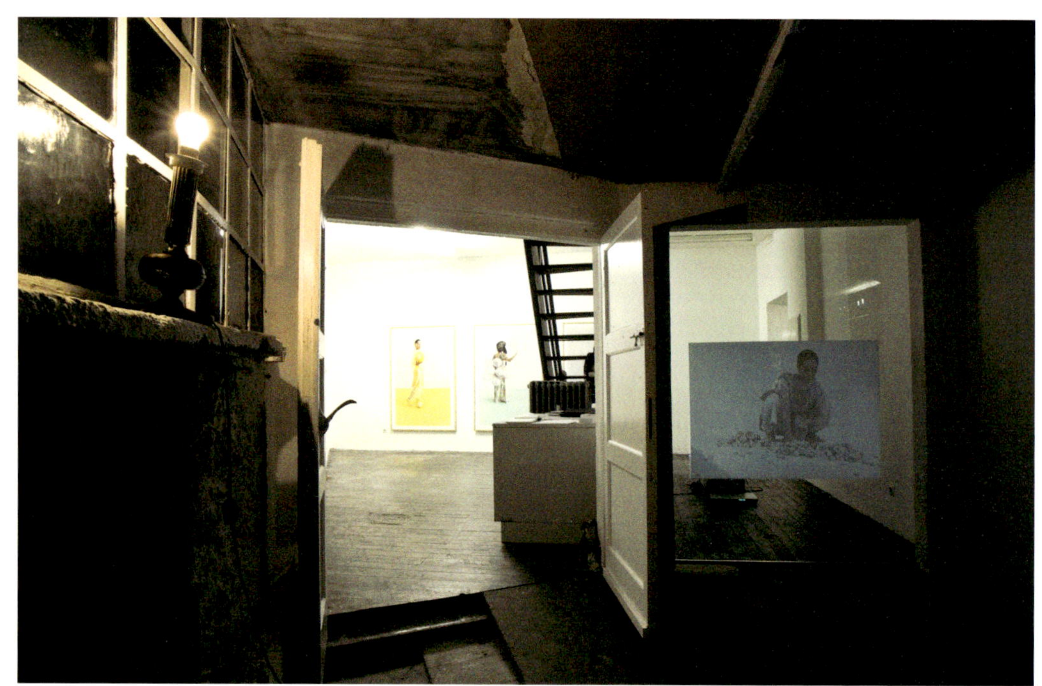

Contemporär Galerie, München, 2005

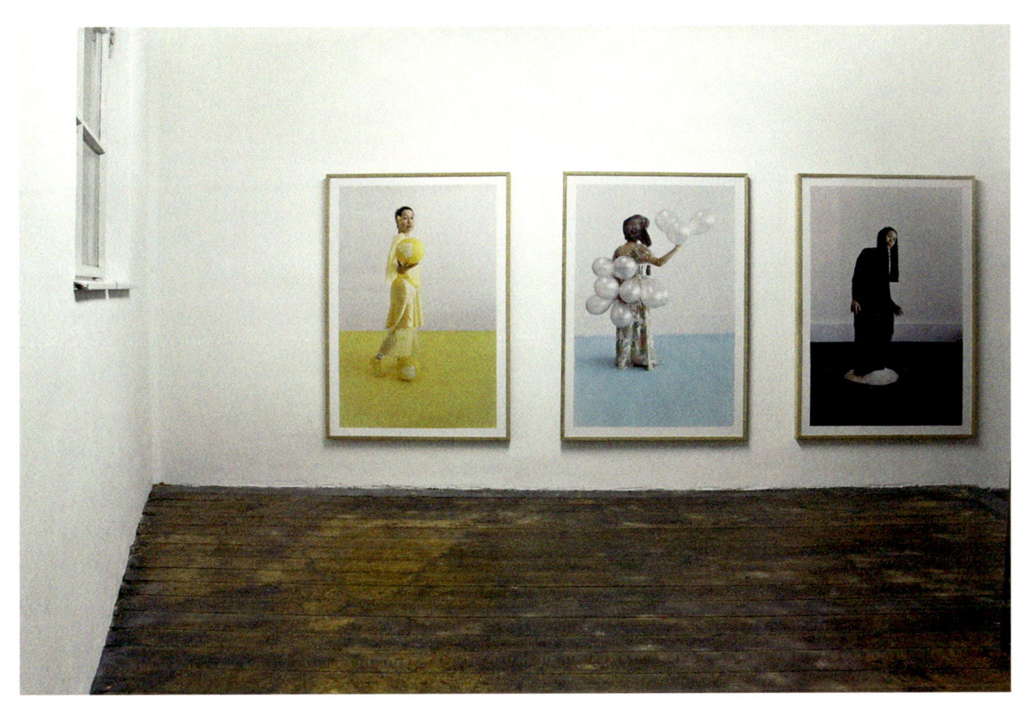

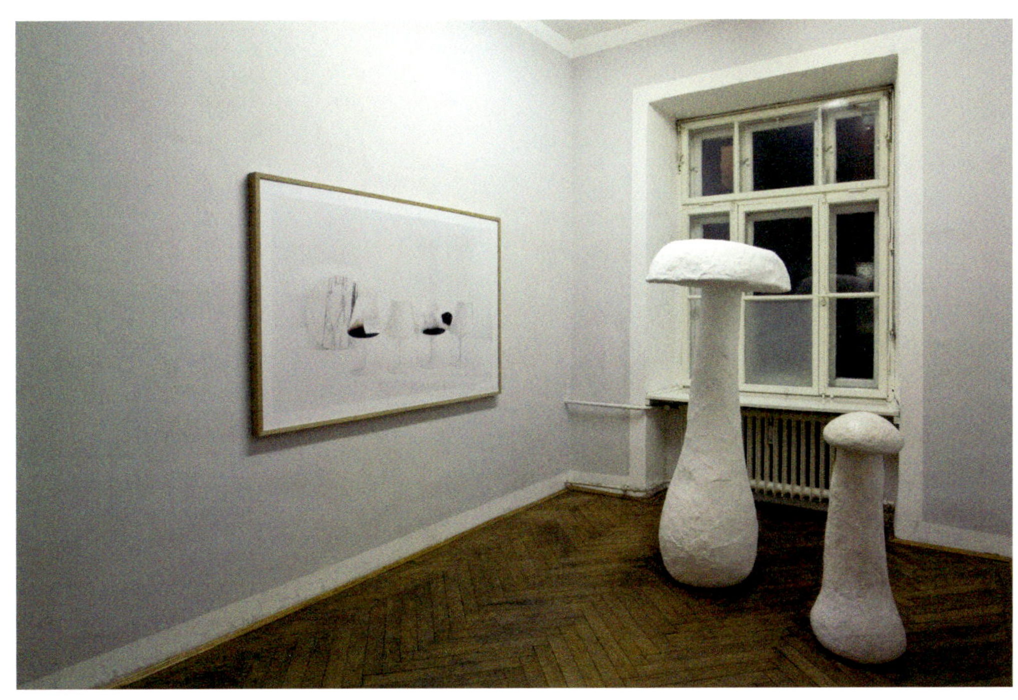

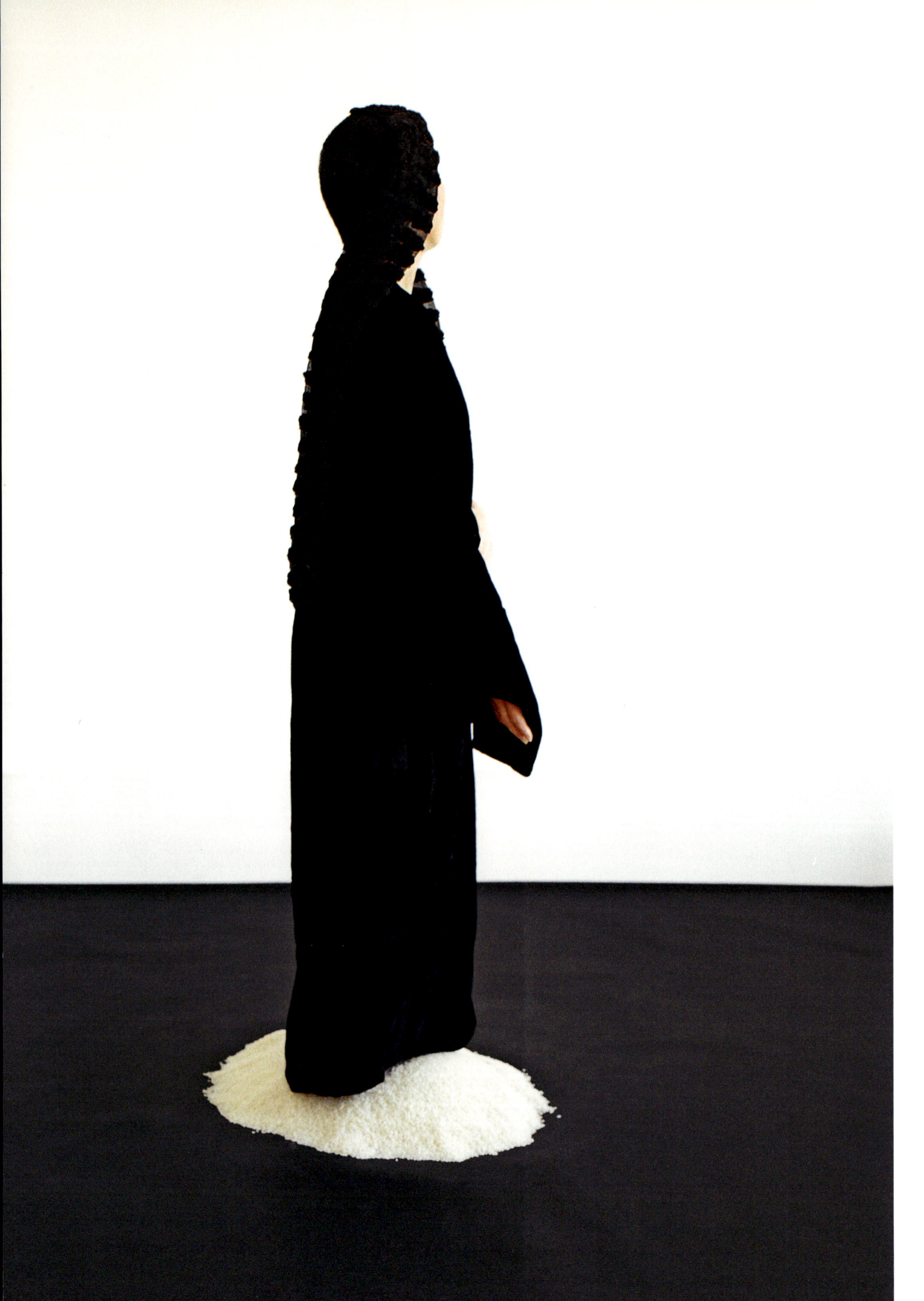

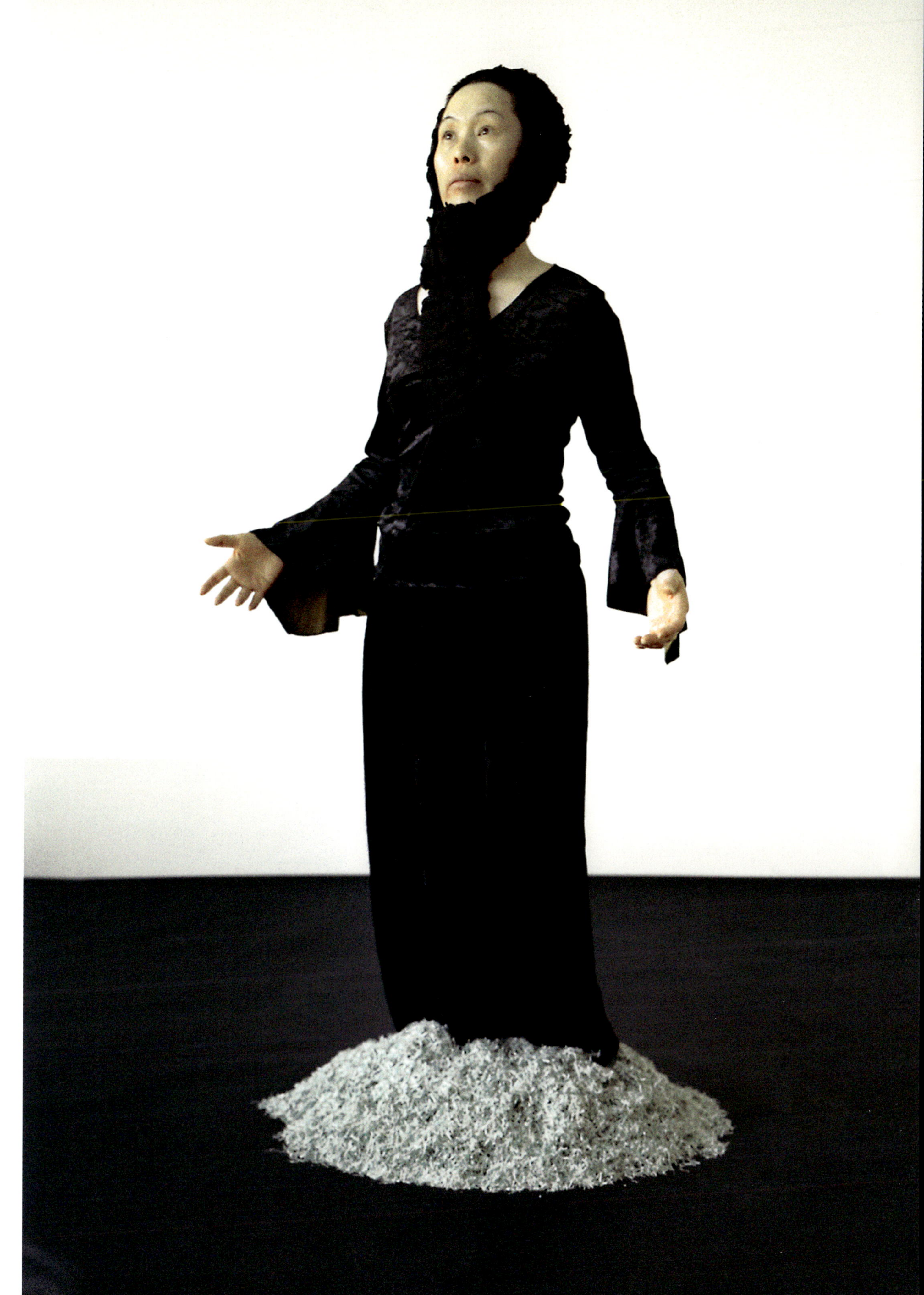

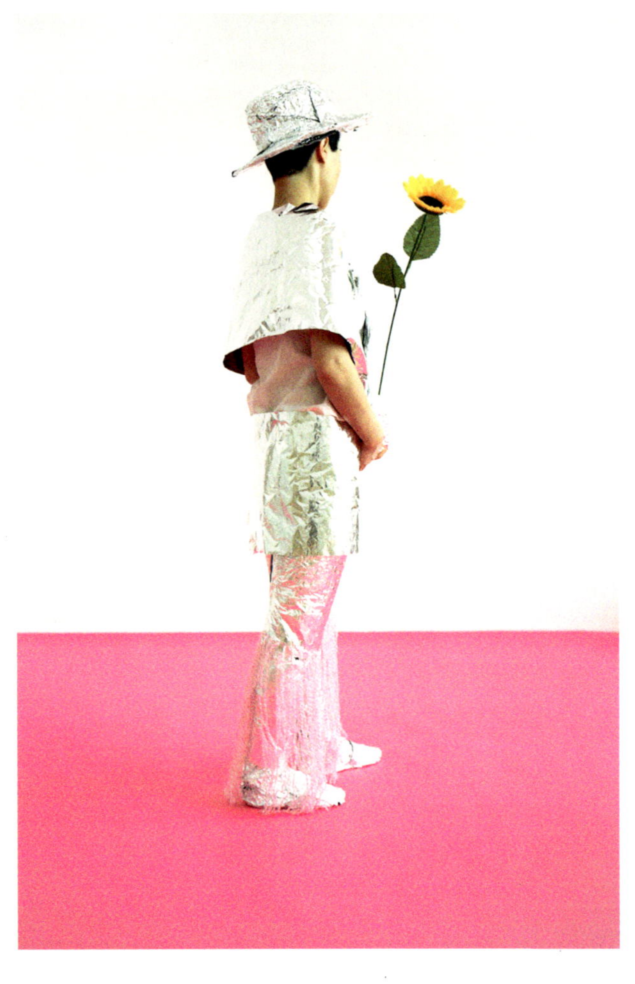

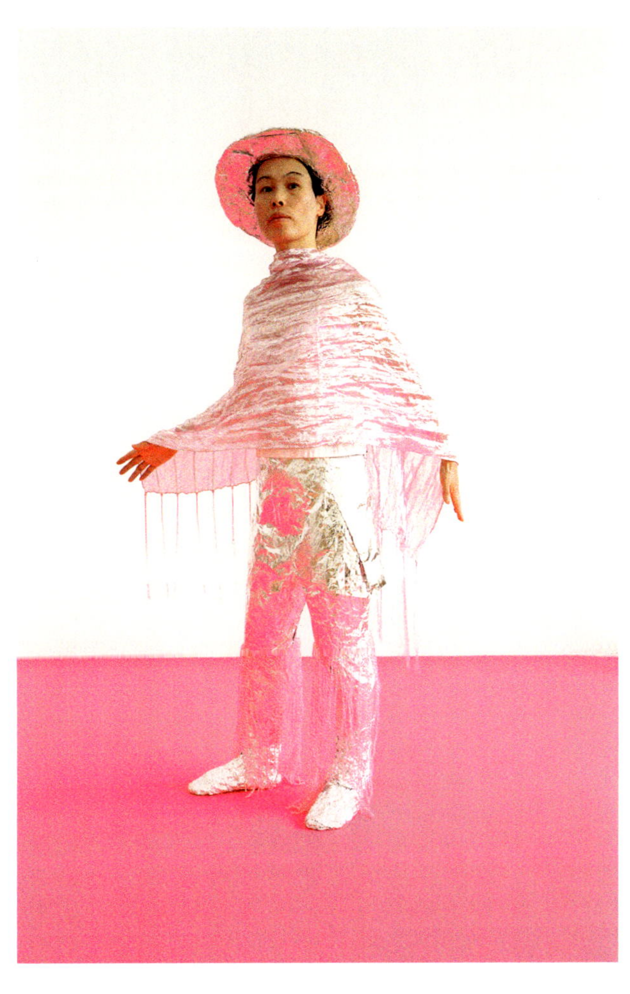

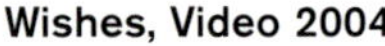
Wishes, Video 2004

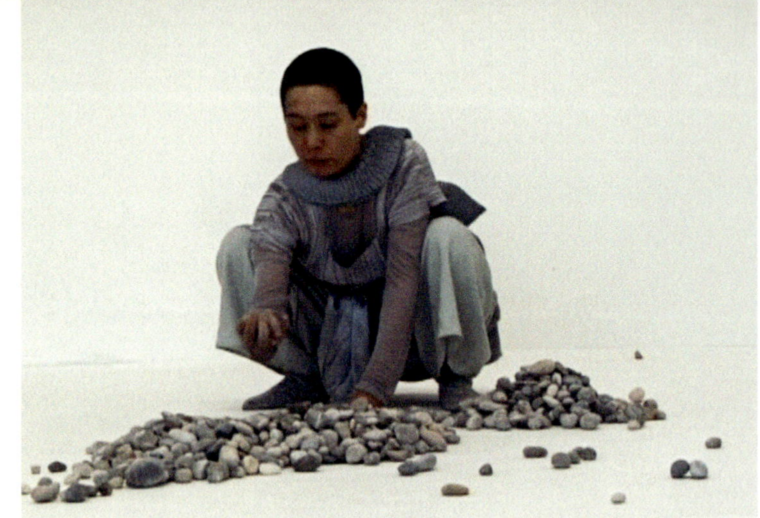

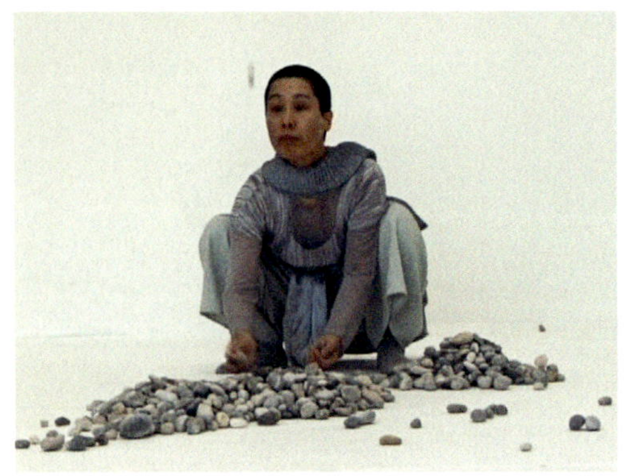

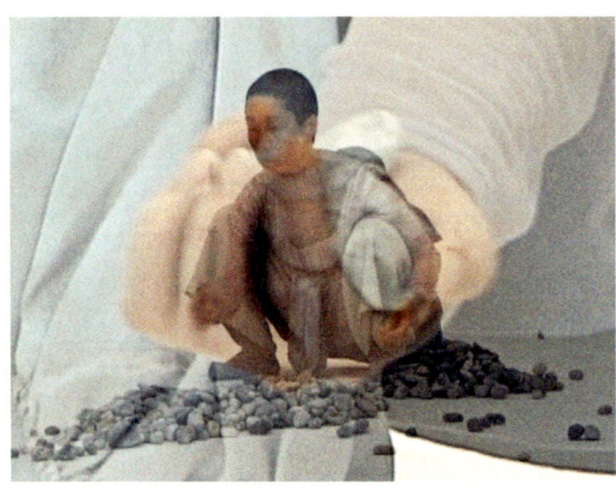

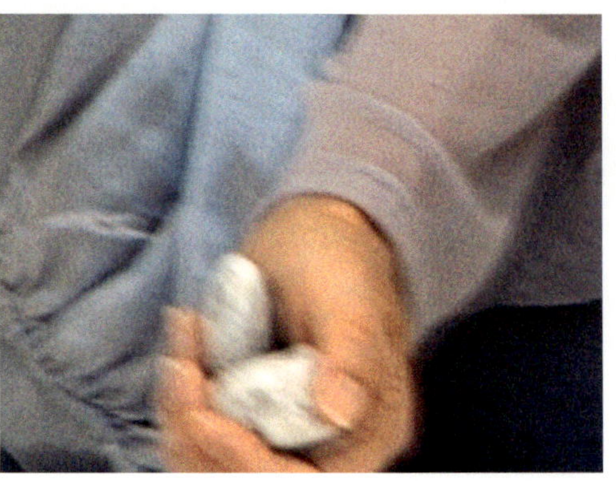

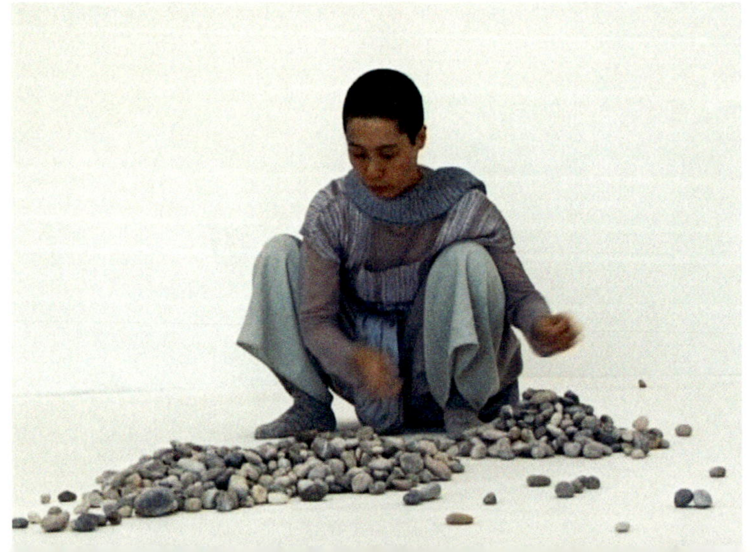

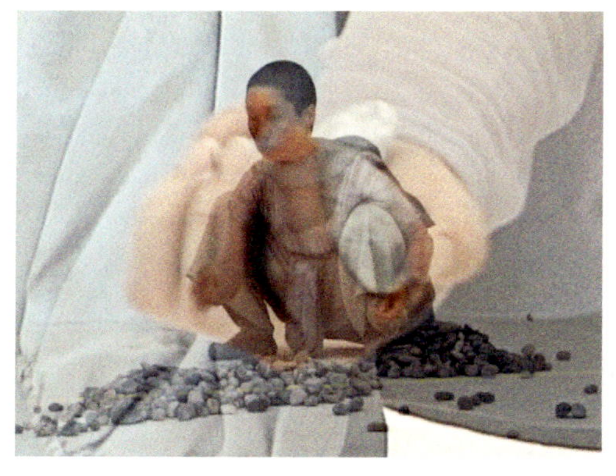
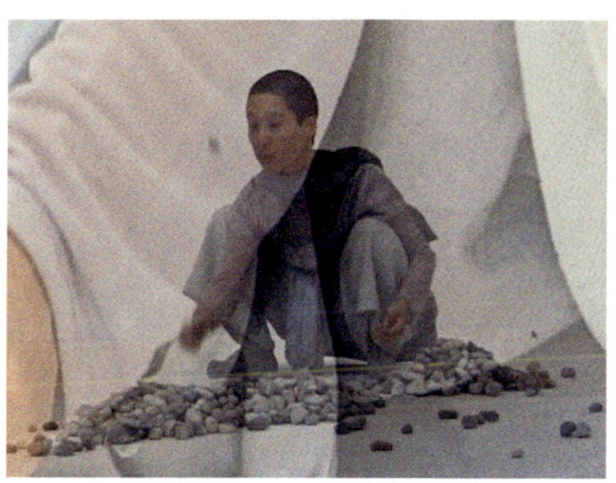
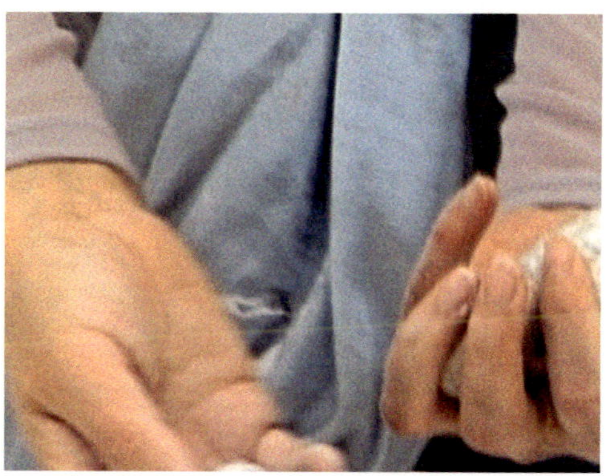
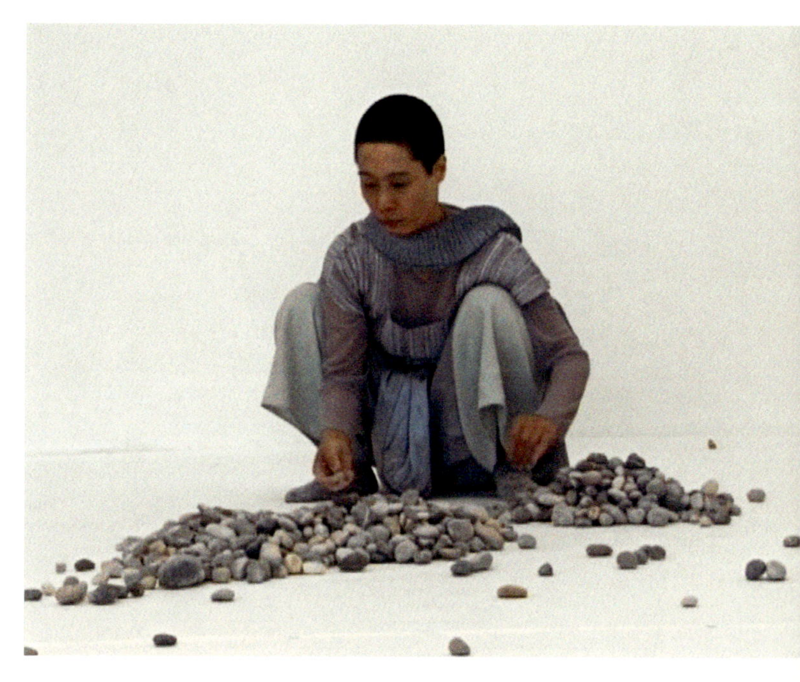

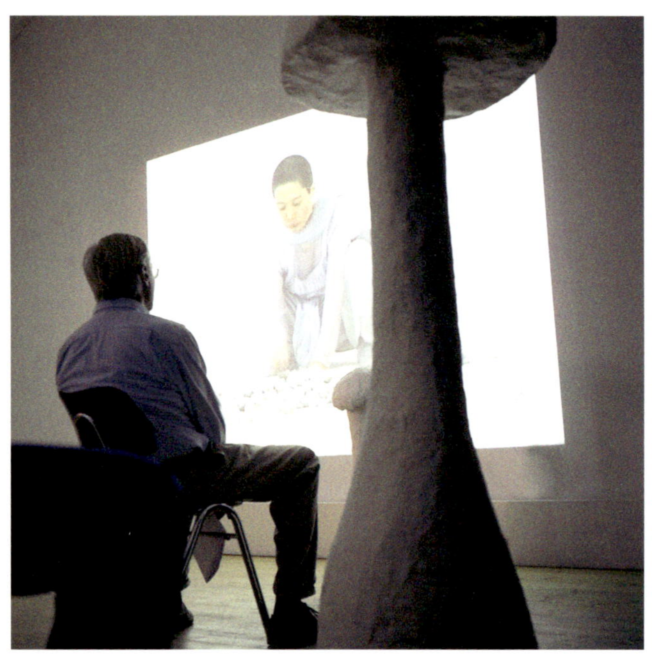

Jahresausstellung Akademie der Bildenden Künste
München, 2004

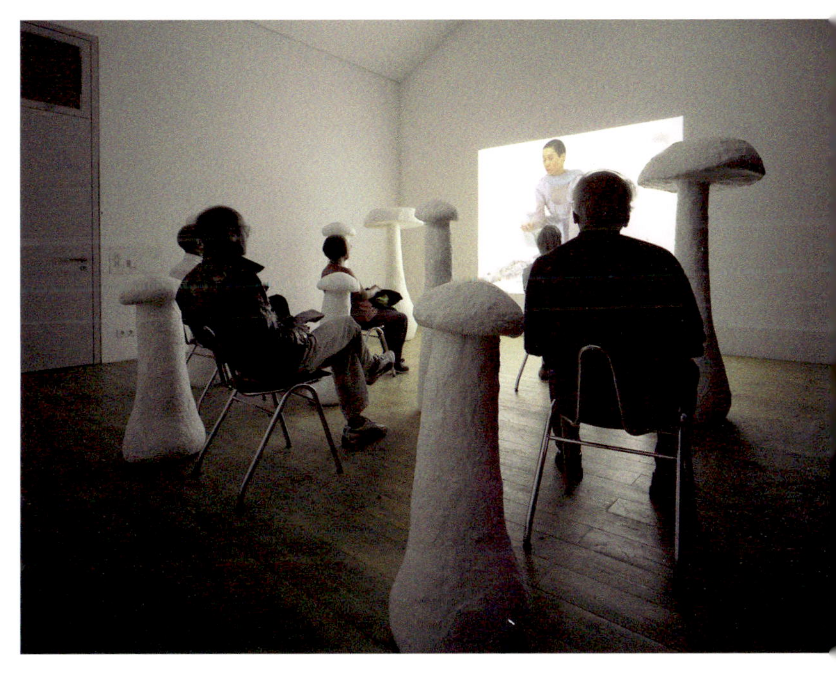

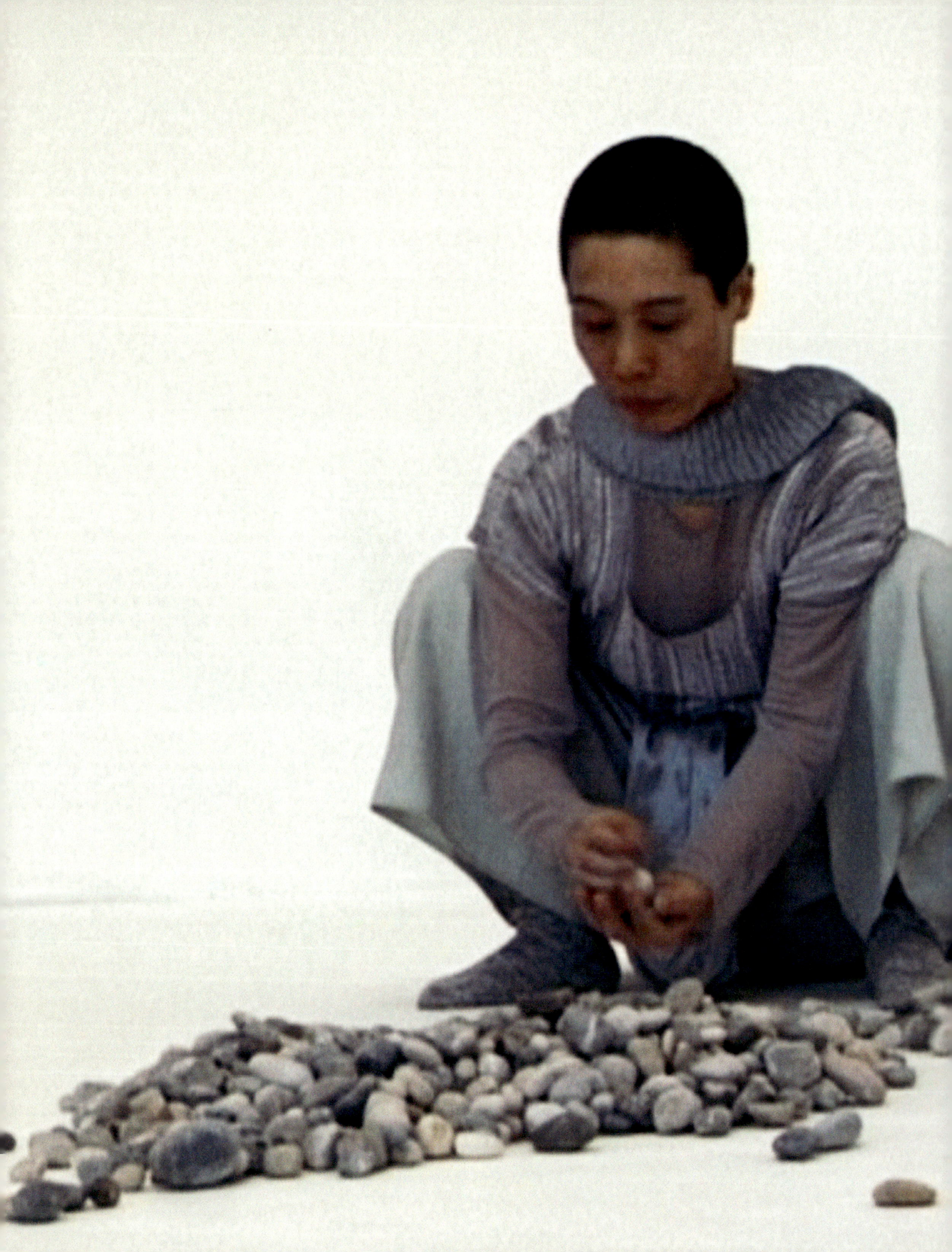

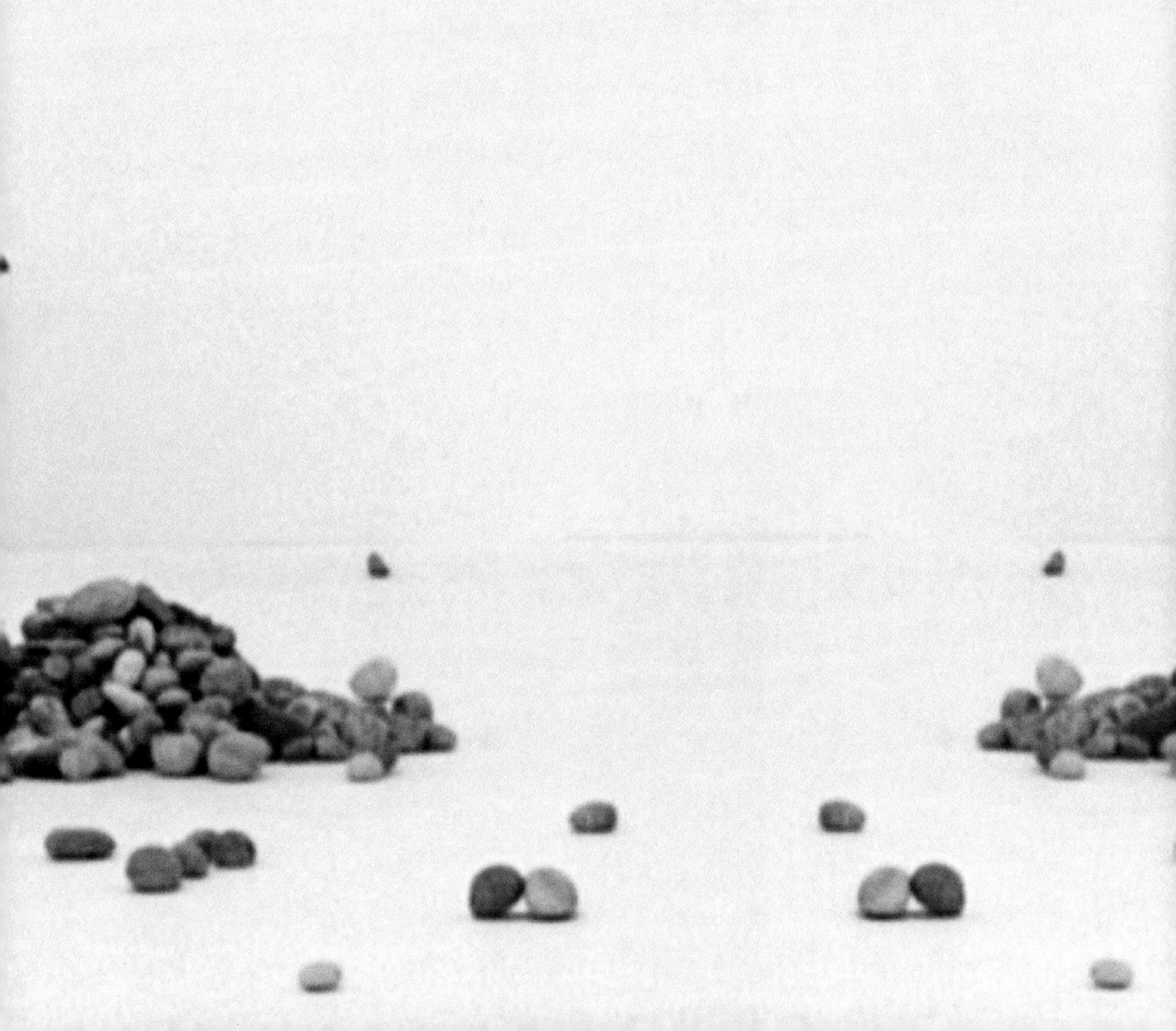

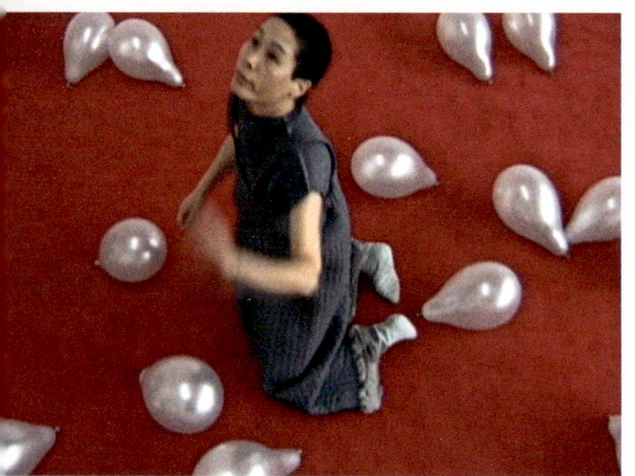

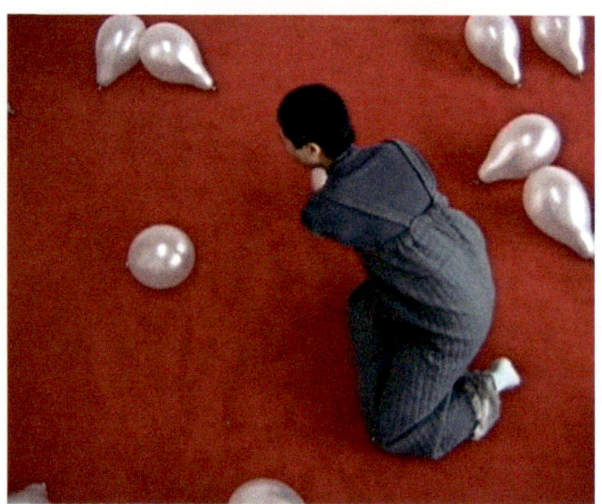

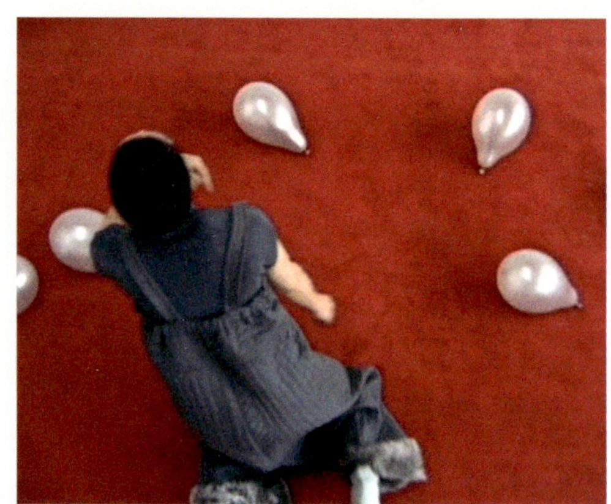

Wishes, Video 2005

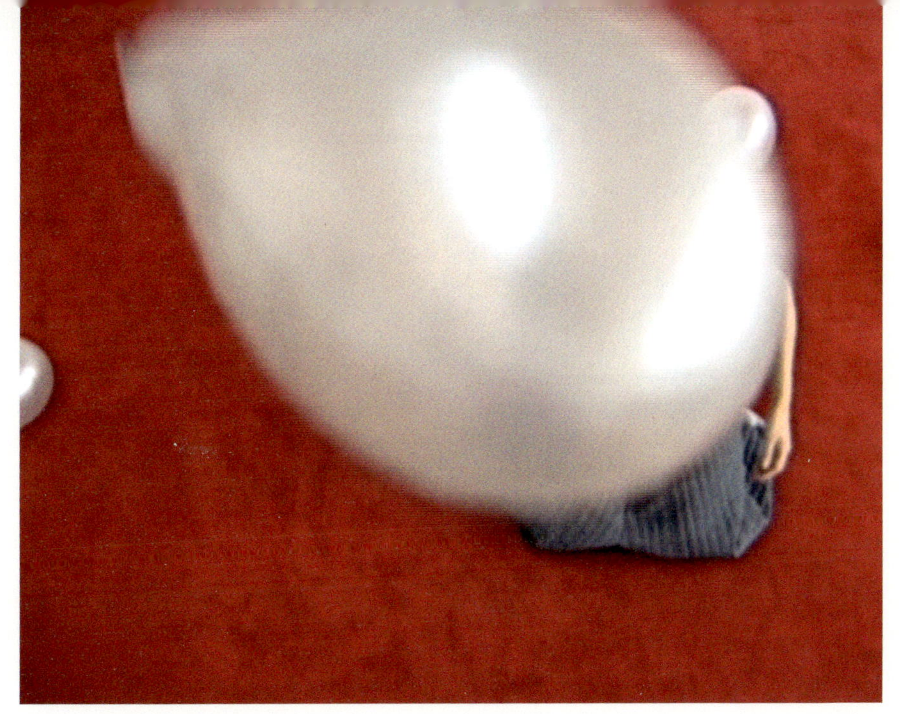

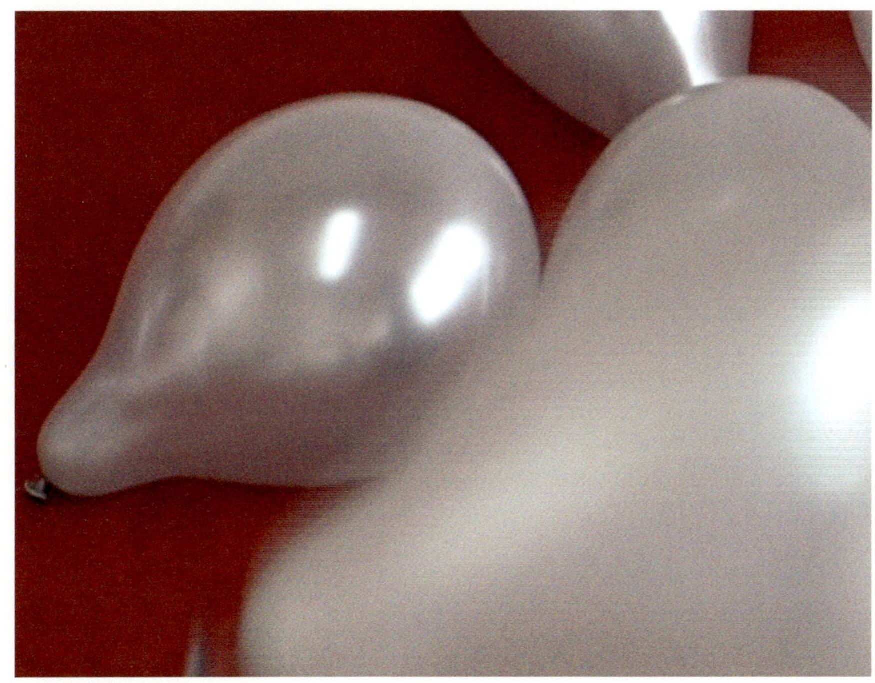

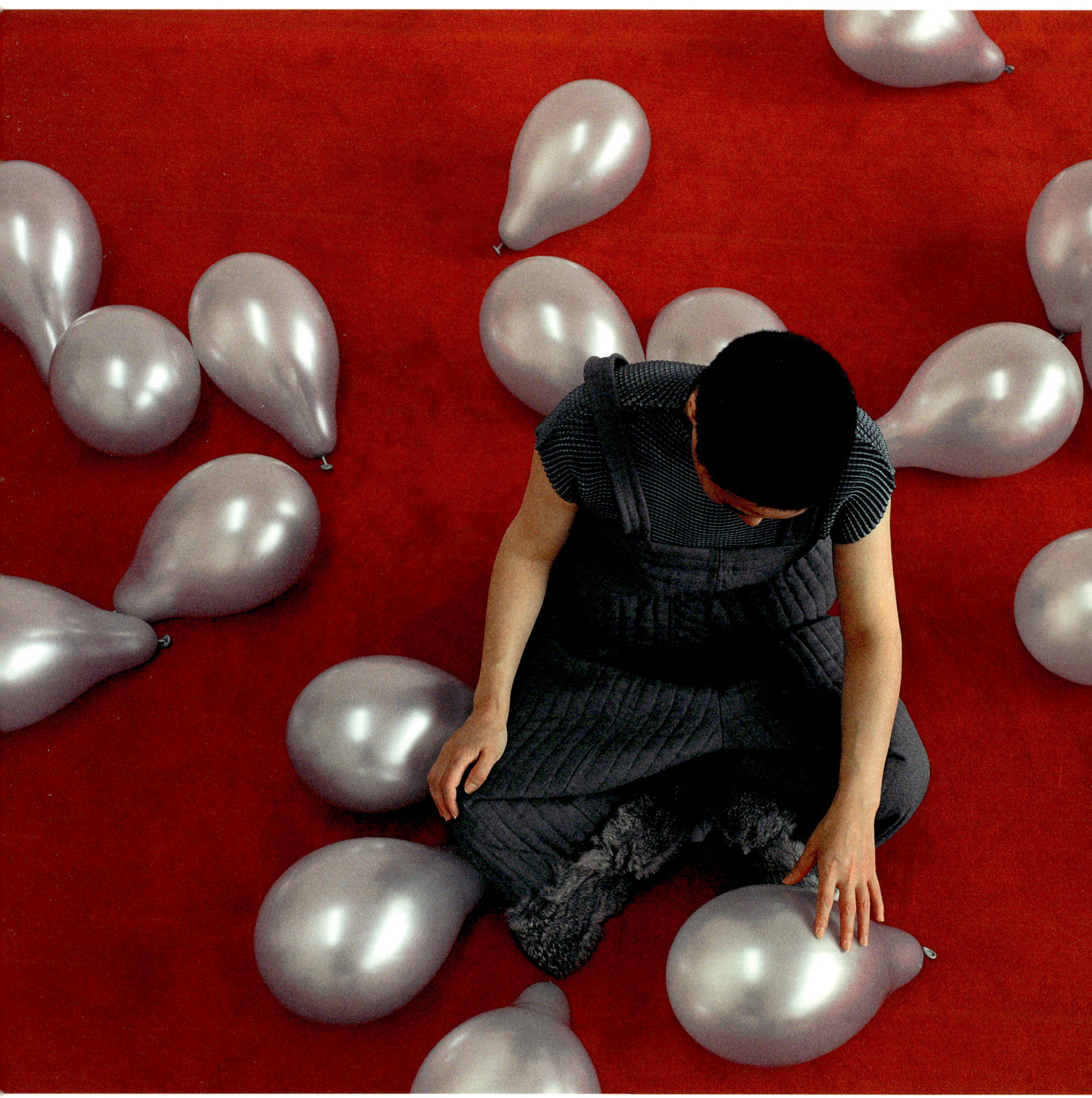

Wishes, 2005

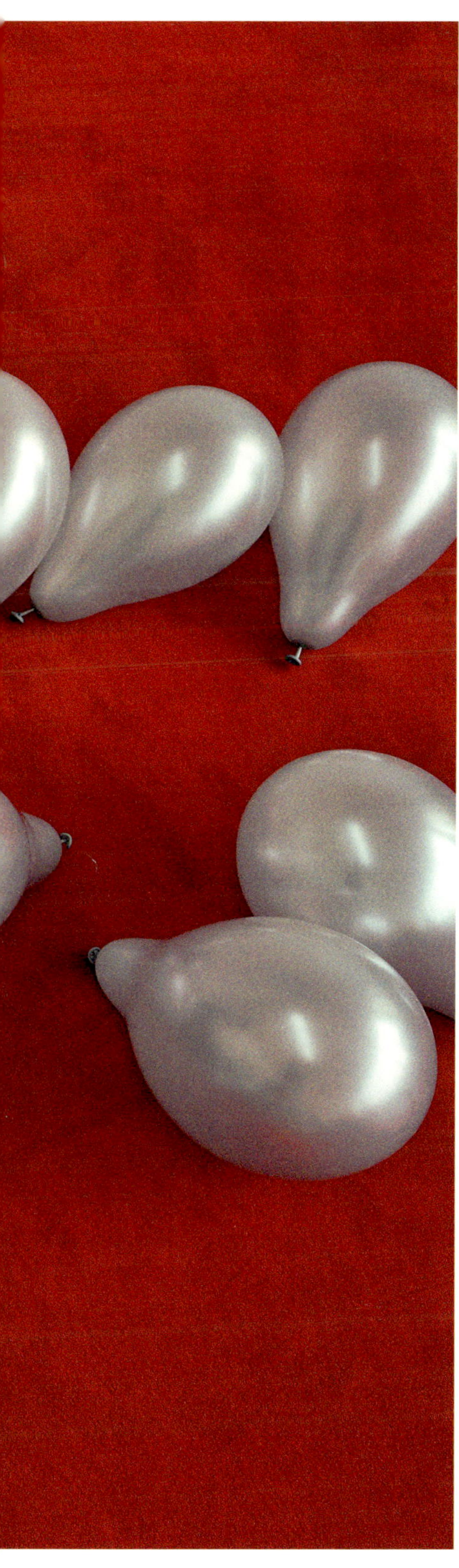

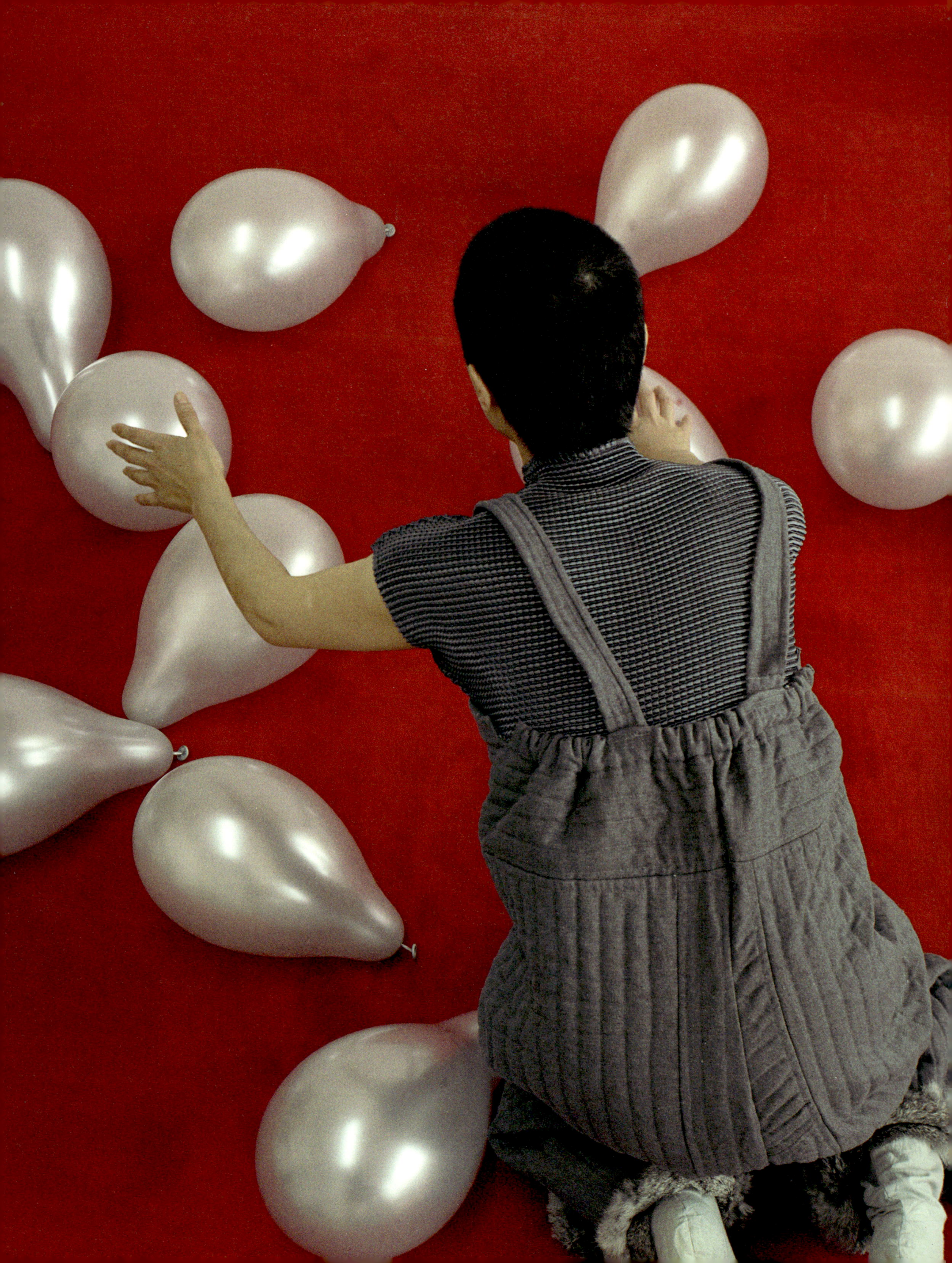

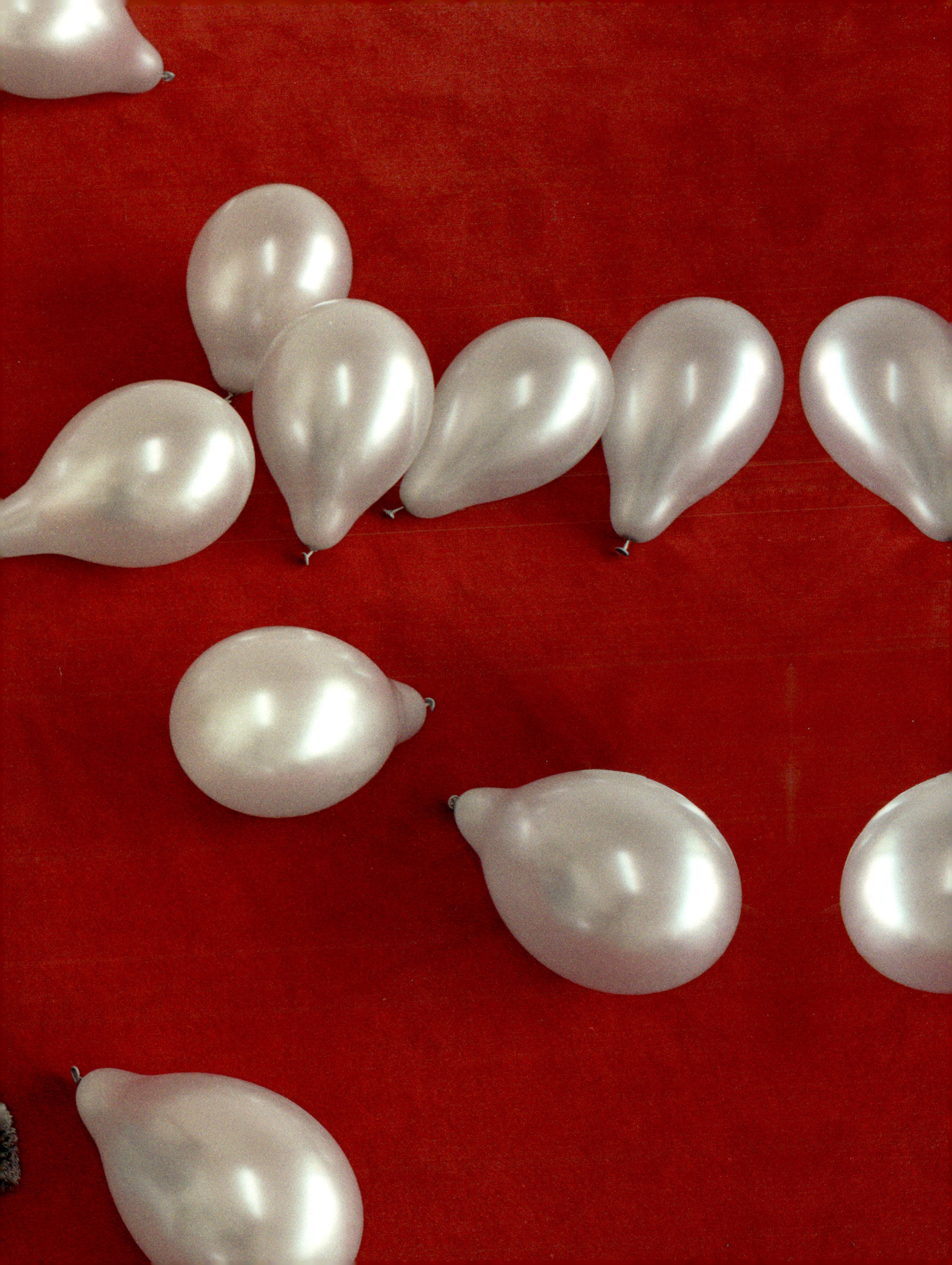

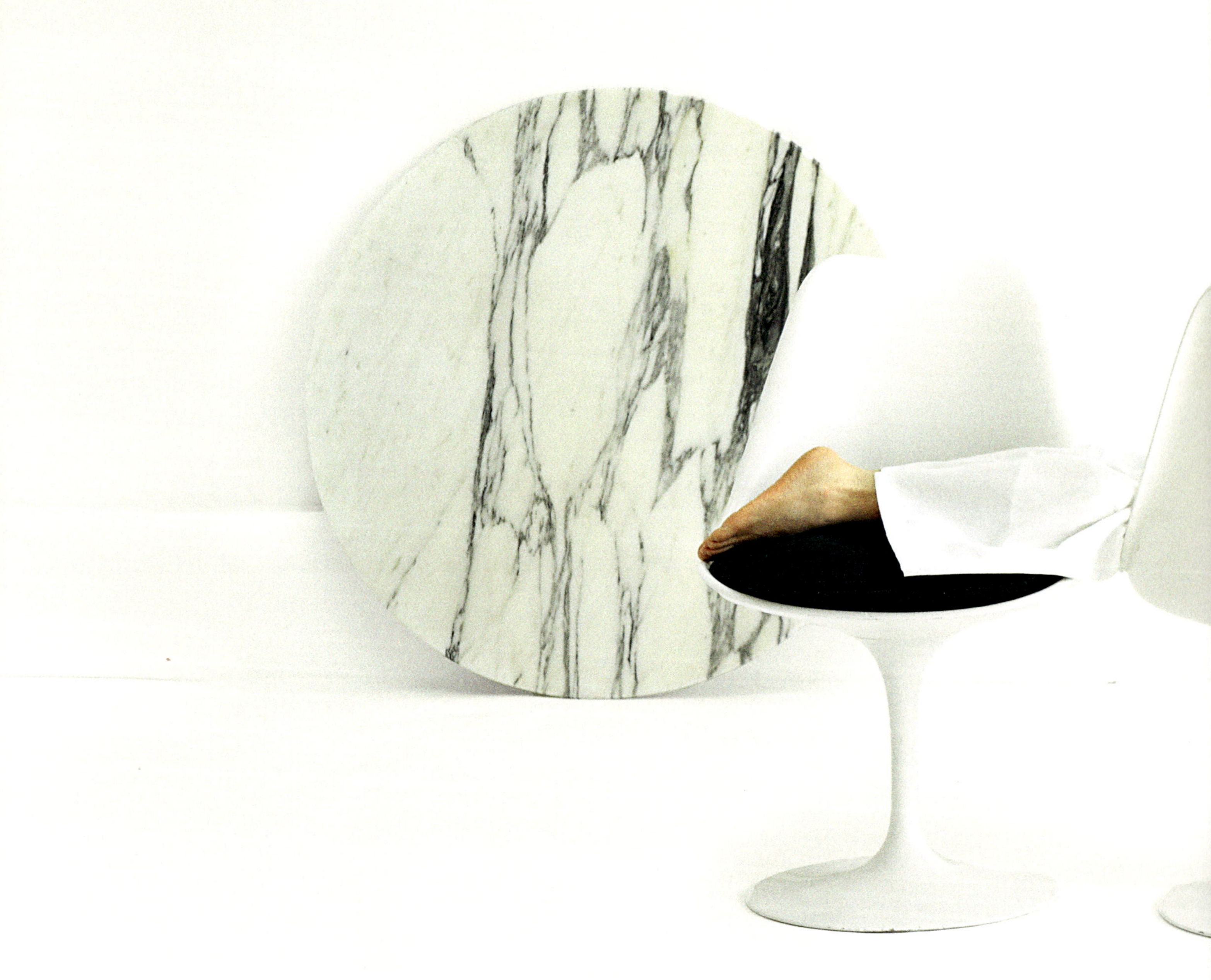

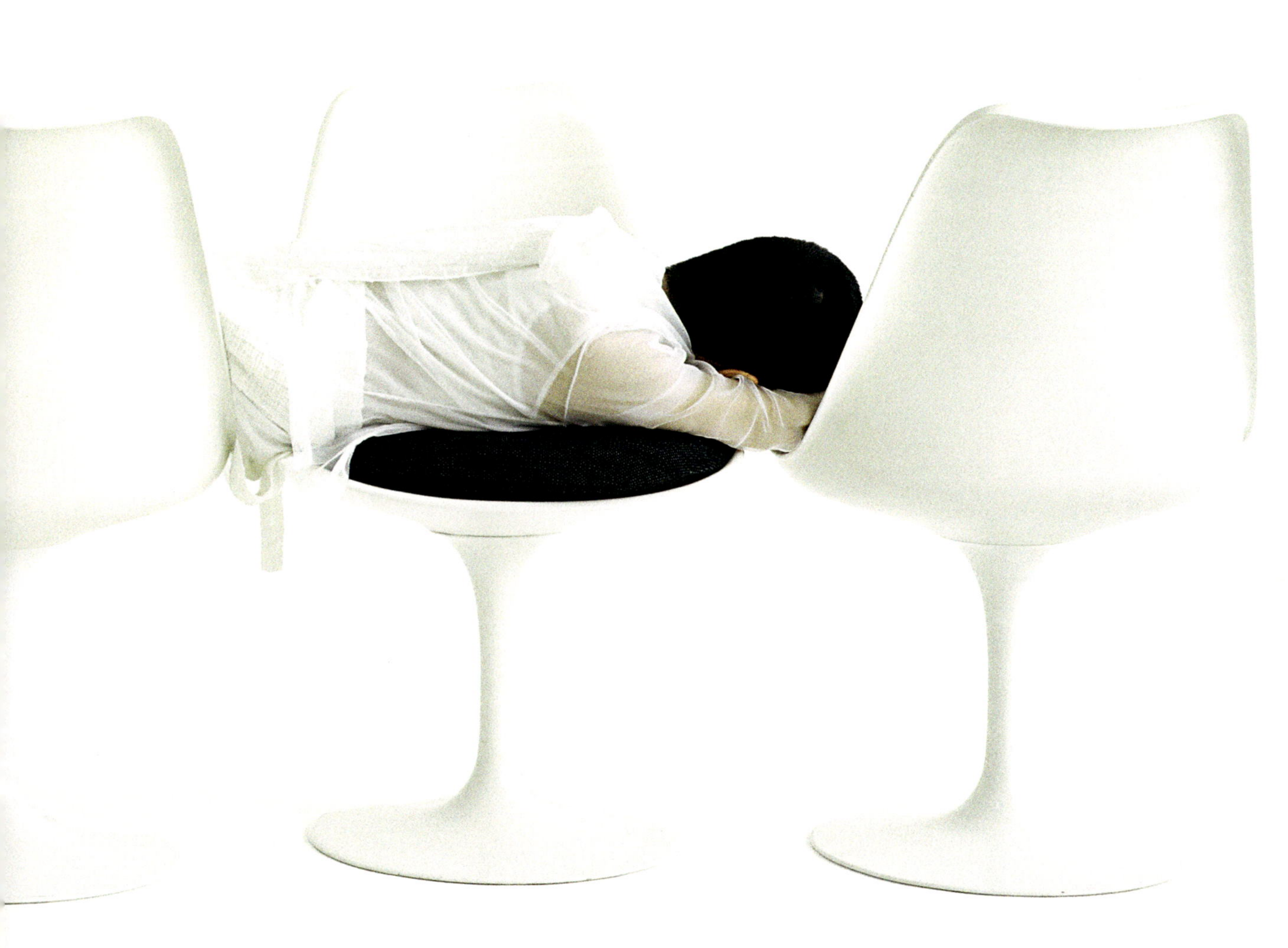

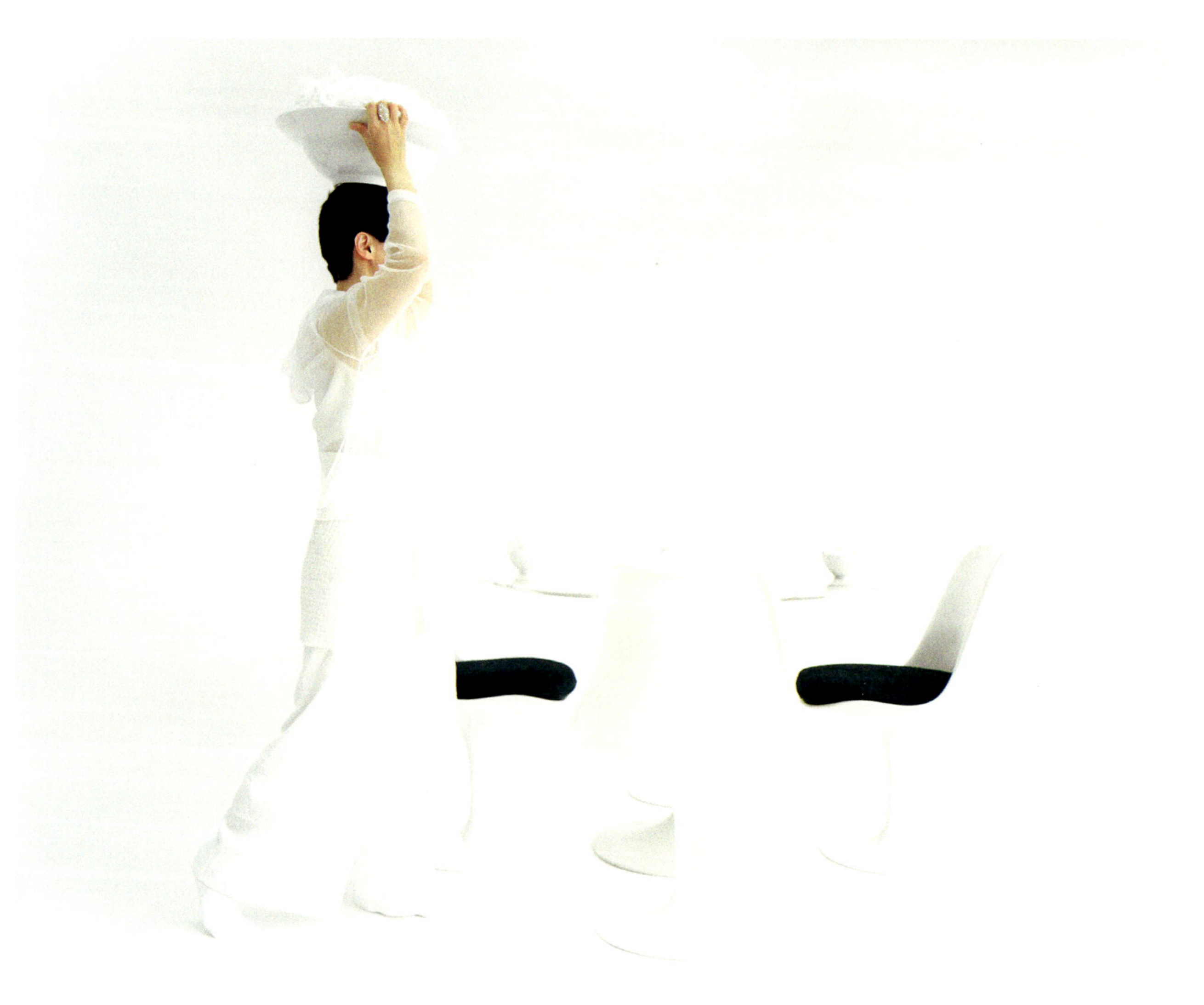

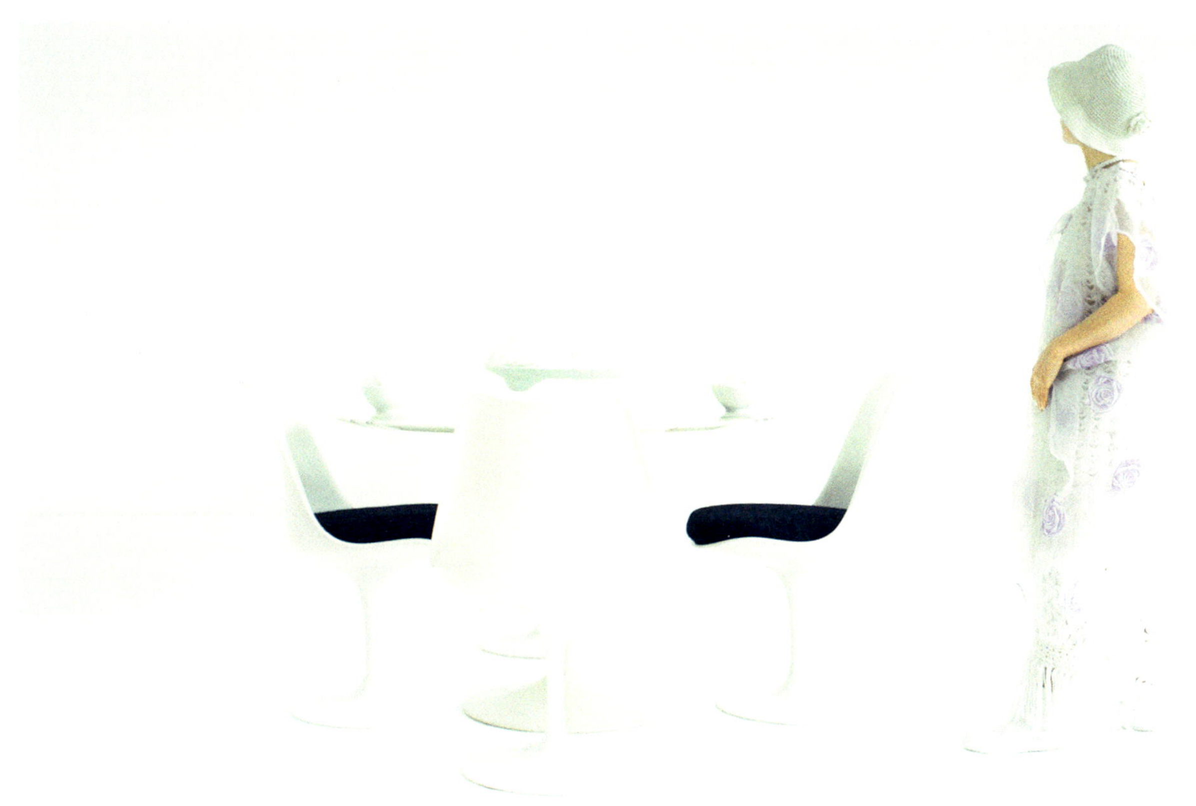

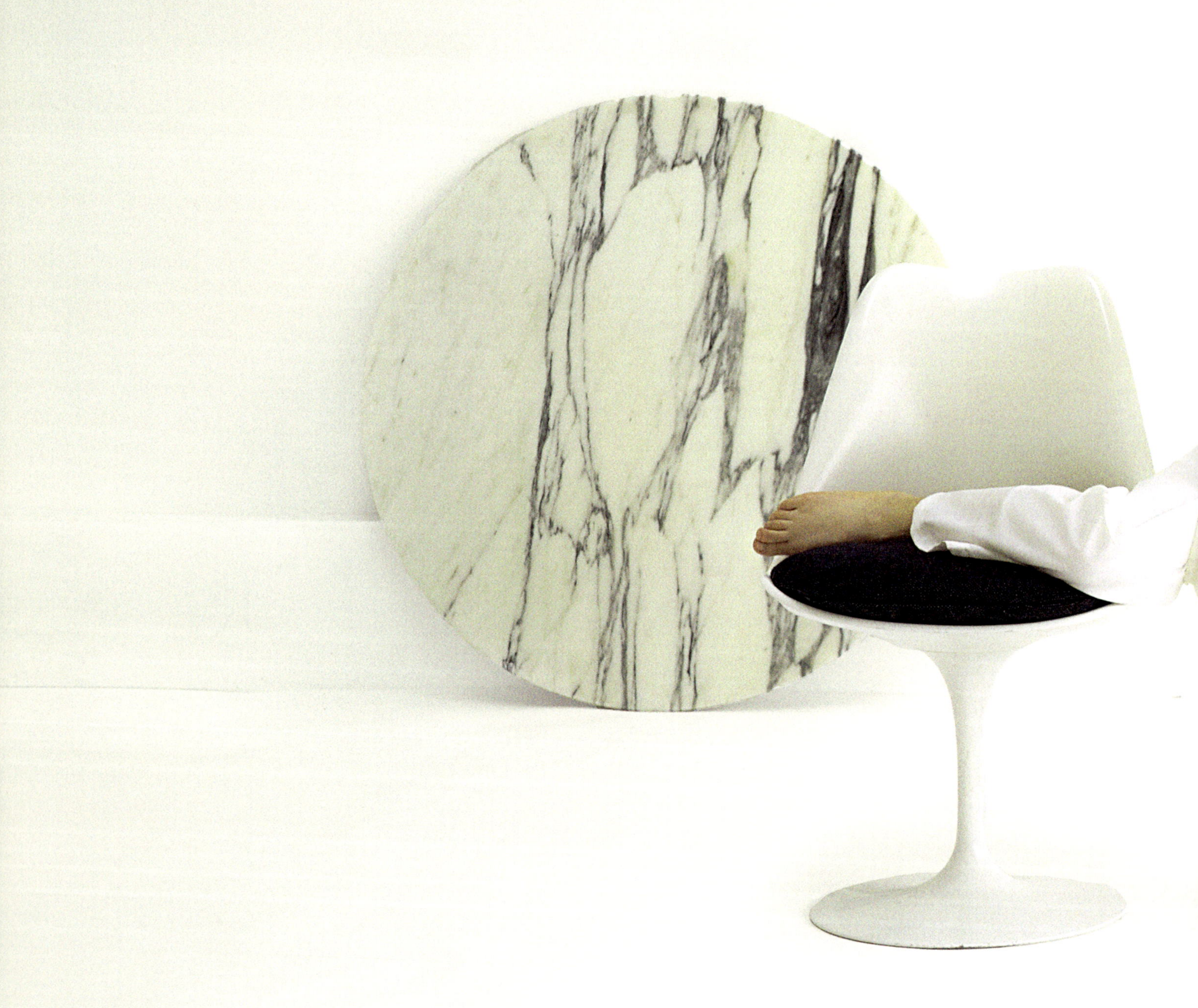

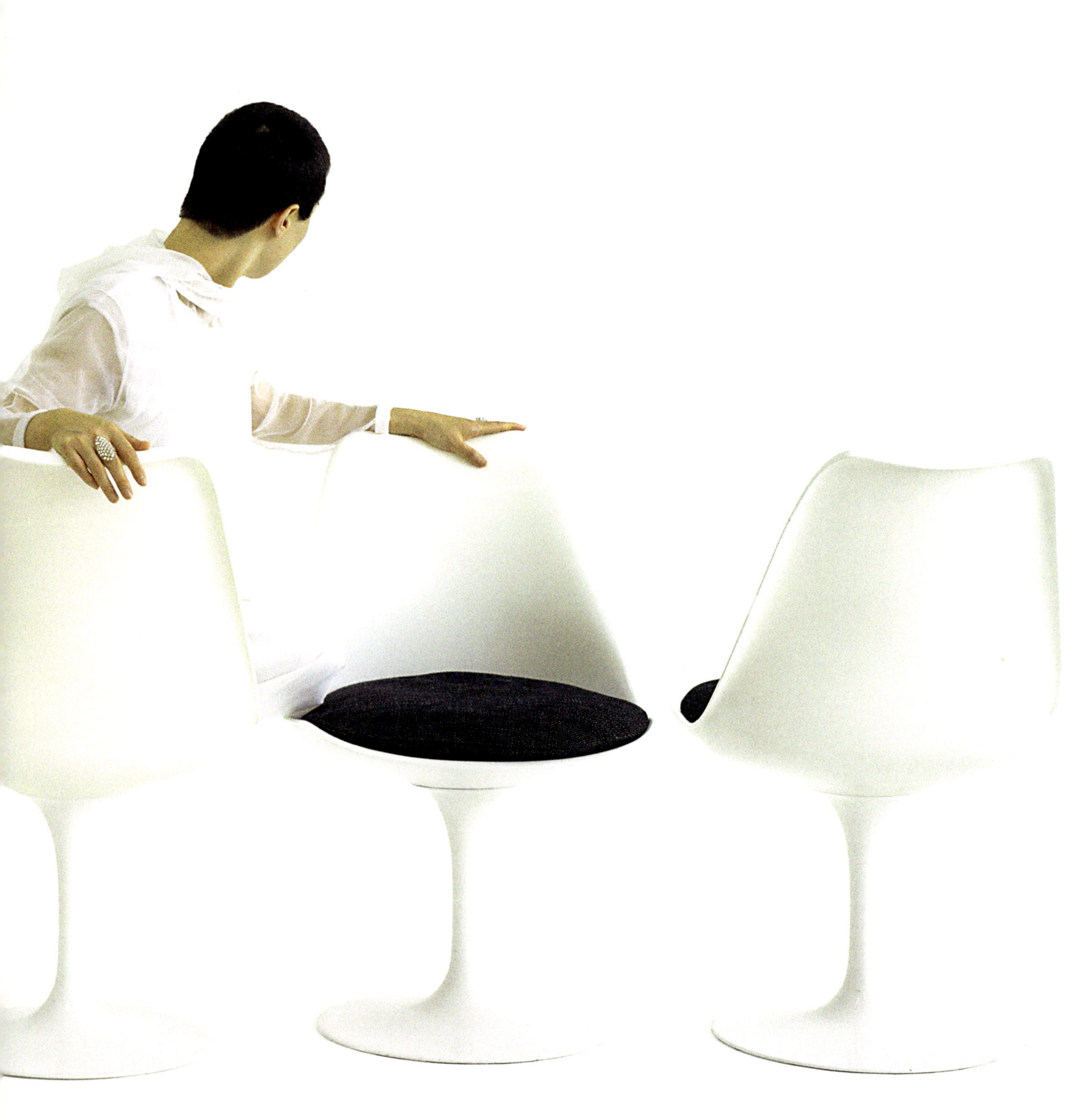

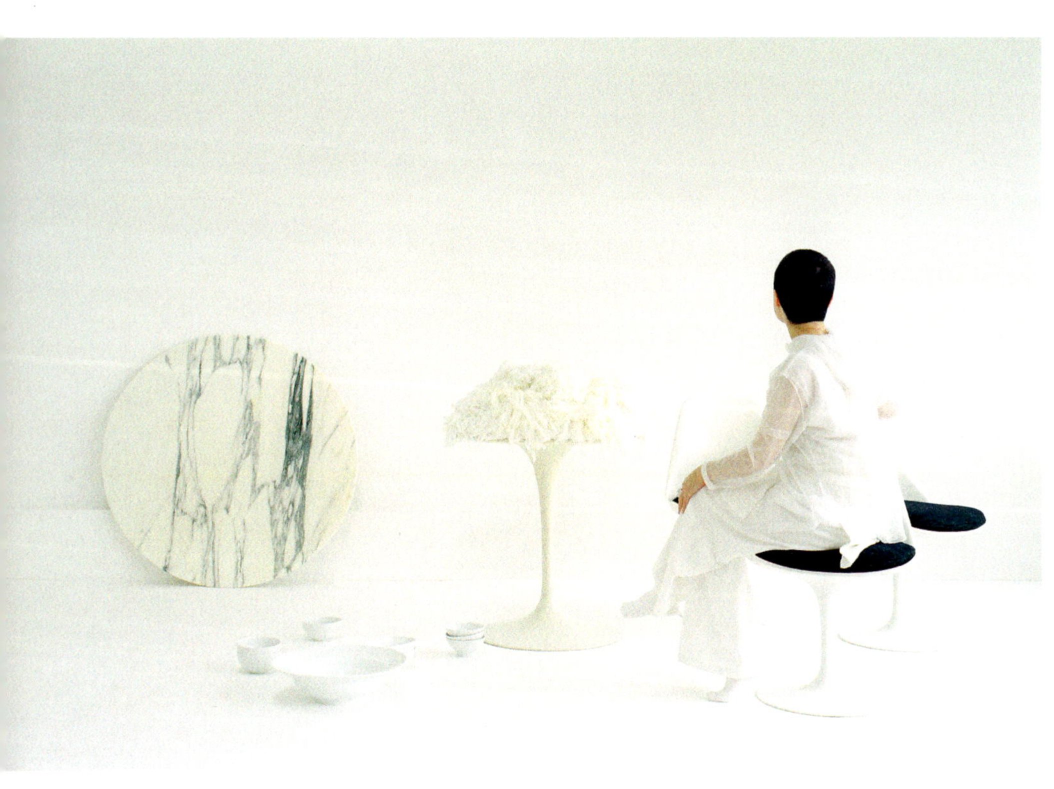

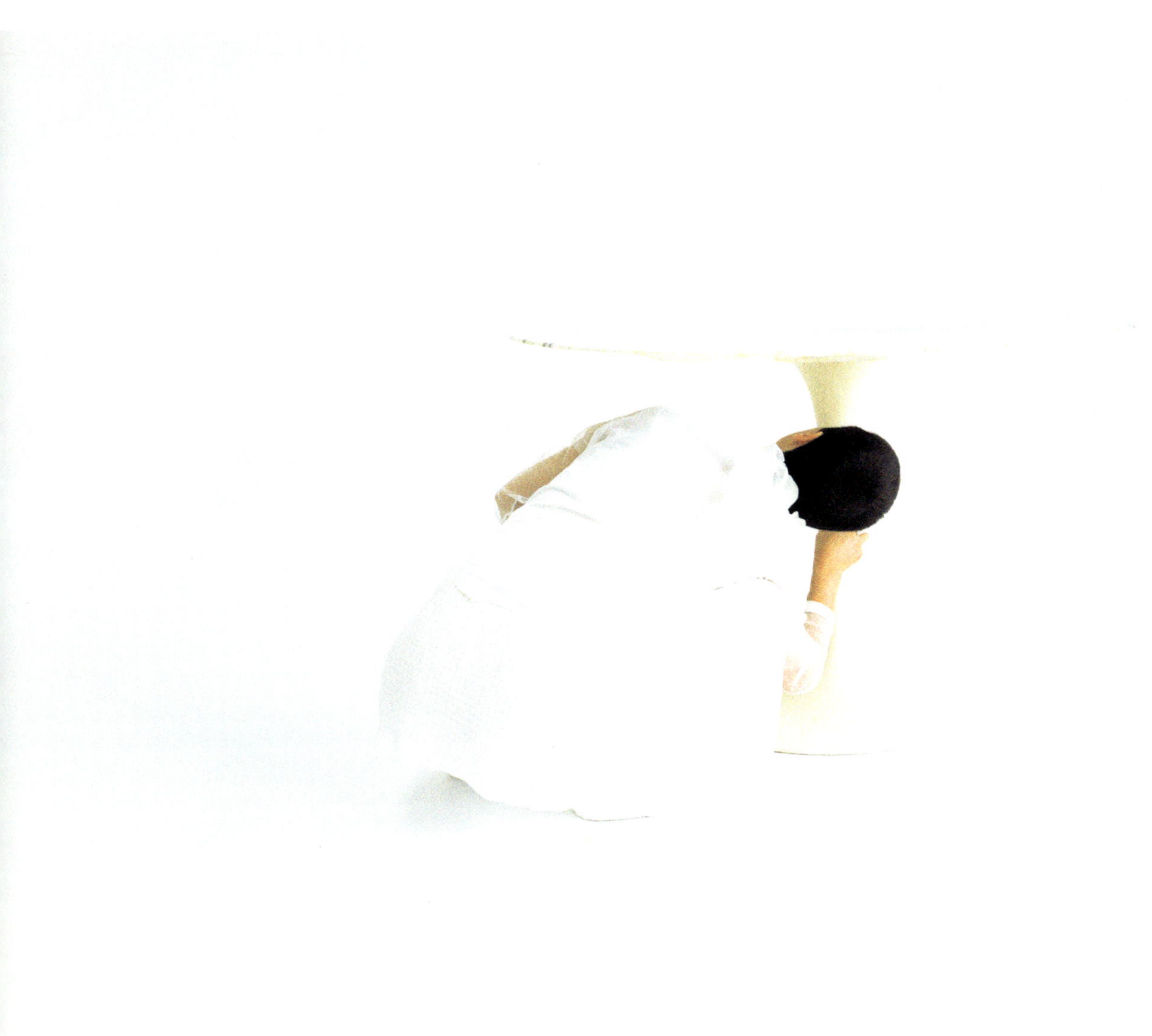

Daniela Zyman

Entortete Bildwelten

Die Betrachtung der fotografischen und filmischen Arbeiten von S'nim Oh wirft die Frage nach der Darstellbarkeit des Selbst in einer von Migration, Fragmentierung, Hybridität gekennzeichneten Kultur auf. Das Selbst, das hier zur Disposition steht, ist nicht das autobiographische Selbst, das zwischen Wahrheit und Fiktion, zwischen Autor und Subjekt laviert und von einem einheitlichen, geschlossenen, daher universalistischen Repräsentationsregime definiert wird. S'nim Ohs Arbeiten zeigen, dass die Erarbeitung einer Subjektdarstellung, die jene überholten und ausgehöhlten Vorstellungen von Homogenität hinter sich lassen, eine der anstehenden Herausforderung von zeitgenössischen KünstlerInnen ist.

Identität ins Spiel zu bringen bedeutet mehr, als das Ich ins Bild zu bringen. Es berührt zwangsläufig auch die internen Probleme der Repräsentation und Kommunikation. Es berührt die Frage nach dem »Wesen« oder dem »Ort« der Kultur. Wie lässt sich die tradierte Hegemonie westlicher Darstellungsmodi und ihr formalisiertes Regelwerk für eine Neuformulierung reappropriieren, ohne dass das neu gewonnene Territorium zu einem reinem Genre wird? Mit welchen Denk- und Darstellungsfiguren operieren KünstlerInnen wie S'nim Oh um komplexe Bildformen zu schaffen, die (auch) die Frage der kulturellen Differenz als produktive Desorientierung und nicht als Festschreibung einer vereinnehmbaren Andersartigkeit verhandeln?

Die hier angesprochene kulturelle Differenz möchte ich im Sinne Homi Bhabhas und anderer als Überschneidung und Überlappung jener Teilaspekte, die Identität heute bestimmen – also anhand der divergierenden Zugehörigkeiten zu kulturellen, klassen-, ort-, und geschlechtsspezifischen symbolischen Verknotungen und nicht als ethnische Position definieren – also mittels S'nim Ohs ethnischem Ursprung als Koreanerin. Die Fragestellung der Individualisierung in Folge von kultureller Differenz und »Entortung« birgt die Möglichkeiten eines narrativen Potenzials, das die US amerikanisch-koreanische Theoretikerin Miwon Kwon in ihrem Artikel »Imagining an Impossible World Picture«, wie folgt beschreibt: »It may be more comforting to perceive and/or imagine oneself in relation to a cohesive whole, be it a city or a more abstract social structure. But it seems to me that individual self-recognition, which is the fundamental basis for the possibilities of a collective formation, is not a continuous state of consciousness, but rather a scattered, messy desire based on infrequent and unpredictable moments of epiphanous realizations of one's subjectivity. It is not through a continuous accumulation of partial mental pictures or memories of familiar spaces/social realities that one consolidates or grounds one's sense of place/self. Instead, it is through the very shock of ruptures, incongruencies, and discontinuities that one is reminded (in negation) of the sense of wholeness and place. For me, it was precisely at the moment of recognizing my own erasure that I imagined myself as a social subject within an impossible world picture.« [1]

Das Interessante an dieser Beschreibung Kwons und ihrer weiteren theoretischen Formulierung der »condition of ungrounded transience« ist die Vorstellung, dass Identität zunehmend abgelöst von einem fixen Begriff von Örtlichkeit, Heimat und Selbst erzählbar und darstellbar ist. Diese Loslösung ist aber auch gekennzeichnet von Verbundenheit und Verlust und von der Notwendigkeit das Verlorene als Unwiederbringbares zu figurieren. Durchlässigkeit und Impermanenz, aber auch das Gefühl von Verbundenheit und dessen Verarbeitung möchte ich S'nim Ohs Arbeiten zuschreiben. »Meine Welt ist unaussprechlich«, »Schein und Wirklichkeit«oder »Wishes« verweisen auf eine Unaussprechbarkeit, die zu gleichen Massen Doppelung (Schein / Wirklichkeit – Welt / unaussprechlich – Wunsch) und Wirklichkeitsbezug (Welt / Wirklichkeit) vereinen.

S'nim Oh verwendet Formen der imaginierten Ent- und Verortung, die die Möglichkeit ständiger prozessualer Refigurierungen bergen. Diese finden primär im Territorium des Selbst statt, also auf der Oberfläche eines performativ wandelnden Selbstbildes jenseits des Altvertrauten. S'nim Ohs ins Bild gebrachte Persona ist von jener Ambivalenz geprägt, die die Zugehörigkeit zu einem heimisch-vertrauten Weltbild durch Doppellungen, Vervielfältigungen, Differenzen sprengt. Diese Doppelung ist allerdings nicht als Grenzziehung zwischen Innen und Außen, zwischen Selbst und Unraum zu lesen, da die vom hybriden Subjekt vorgeführte Intervention und Invention Innen und Außen in gleichen Massen einbezieht. S'nim Ohs Darstellungen und Selbstdarstellungen scheinen nicht nur Innen und Außen gleichermaßen zu erfassen, sondern suggerieren Bildwelten, die nicht dargestellte Momente der Vergangenheit, des Vergangenen imaginieren, Momente, die nicht ins Dispositiv der »großen Erzählungen« gehören, aber die Gegenwart heimsuchen und nach Figuration suchen.

Der für mich gültige Schlüsselbegriff ist in diesem Zusammenhang der Begriff der »Künstlichkeit« im Sinne von Imagination, Verfremdung, Fragmentierung, Doppelung und Aporie. S'nim Ohs fotografische und filmische Arbeit arbeiten mit dem Begriff der Künstlichkeit – »staged images«, fein komponierte szenografische Bilder, die in Gestik, Haltung, Ausdruck, Farbkomposition, Kleidung »hybride Momente« inszenieren. Und doch ist diese Künstlichkeit nicht als Gegensatz zu »Realität« zu verstehen. Durch Beschreibung, Gestaltung und Neuanordnung lässt sich Wirklichkeit formieren – Realität ist niemals neutral, sondern in steter Neuverhandlung. »Die Begriffe ›Verfremdung‹ und Reflexivität stellen nicht mehr bloße Distanzierungstechiken dar, solange die Trennung zwischen ›textuellem Kunstgriff‹ und ›gesellschaftlicher Haltung‹ aufrechterhalten bleiben«. Um mit Trinh T. Minh-Ha weiterzudenken, ließe sich der Begriff von »elsewhere within here«[2] in diesem Zusammenhang verwenden. Die Gleichzeitigkeit von »hier und jetzt« und »Losgelöstheit« und »Anderswo« drückt sehr passend den Zwischenzustand aus, der sowohl örtlich, psychisch, genderspezifisch als auch künstlerisch die Topographie von S'nim Ohs Arbeiten umschreibt.

»Elsewhere within here« öffnet auch den Zugang zum Imaginären, also zu jenem Raum, der durch keine Geschichte voll abgedeckt ist. Es existiert als dazwischen. Das Imaginäre ist die »Ordnung« des nichtsprachlichen Aspektes der Psyche. Es beschreibt die Beziehung zwischen dem Selbst und seinen (unbewussten) Bildern. Dieses Imaginäre bezieht sich nicht nur auf individuelle Phantasien des Unbewussten einzelner Menschen, sondern es gibt Zusammenhänge zu der symbolischen Ordnung, die eine des Kollektivs ist.

»Elsewhere« wird bei S'nim Oh als »Wishes« bezeichnet – Wünsche, die allerdings nicht als »Fiktion«, wie anderorts beschrieben, sondern möglicherweise im Sinne von HYPERLINK »http://de.wikipedia.org/wiki/Ludwig_Wittgenstein« Ludwig Wittgenstein als ein charakteristisches Erlebnis, wie Wiedererkennen, sich erinnern, zu verstehen sind. Die Wünsche, die S'nim Oh beschreibt, liegen anderorts, dazwischen – vielleicht zwischen Westlich/Östlich, Männlich/Weiblich, Hier und Dort, Innen/Außen, Sprache und Handlung, Künstlichkeit/Wirklichkeit, Erinnerung und Verlust, Tradition und Appropriation, Transformation und Erbe. Es ist die ständige Doppelung aller Wertigkeiten, die den konzeptionellen Horizont S'nim Ohs künstlerischer Praxis bilden und uns damit auffordern, Fragen der Repräsentation und Differenz produktiv zu überdenken.

»Because when you talk about difference, there are many ways to receive it; if one simply understands it as a division between culture, between people, between entities, one can't go very far with it. But when that difference between entities is being worked out as a difference also within, things start opening up. Inside and outside are both expanded. Within each entity, there is a vast field and within each self is a multiplicity.«[2]

1 Miwon Kwon, »Imagining an Impossible World Picture«, Lusitania 7 (New York: Lusitania Press, 1995), S. 87.

2 HYPERLINK »http://www.trinhminh-ha.com/« http://www.trinhminh-ha.com/

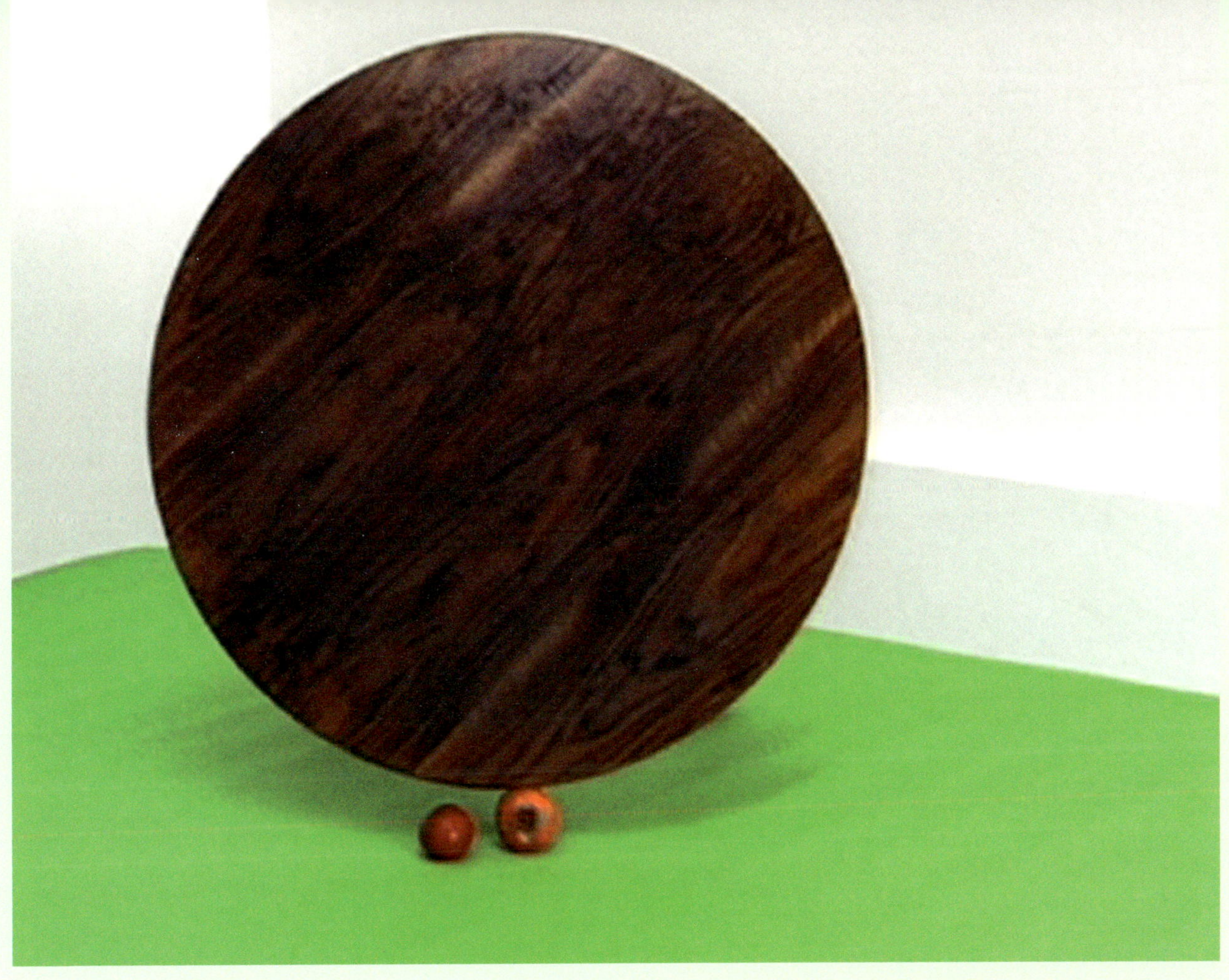

Schein und Wirklichkeit, 2003

Schein und Wirklichkeit, 2003

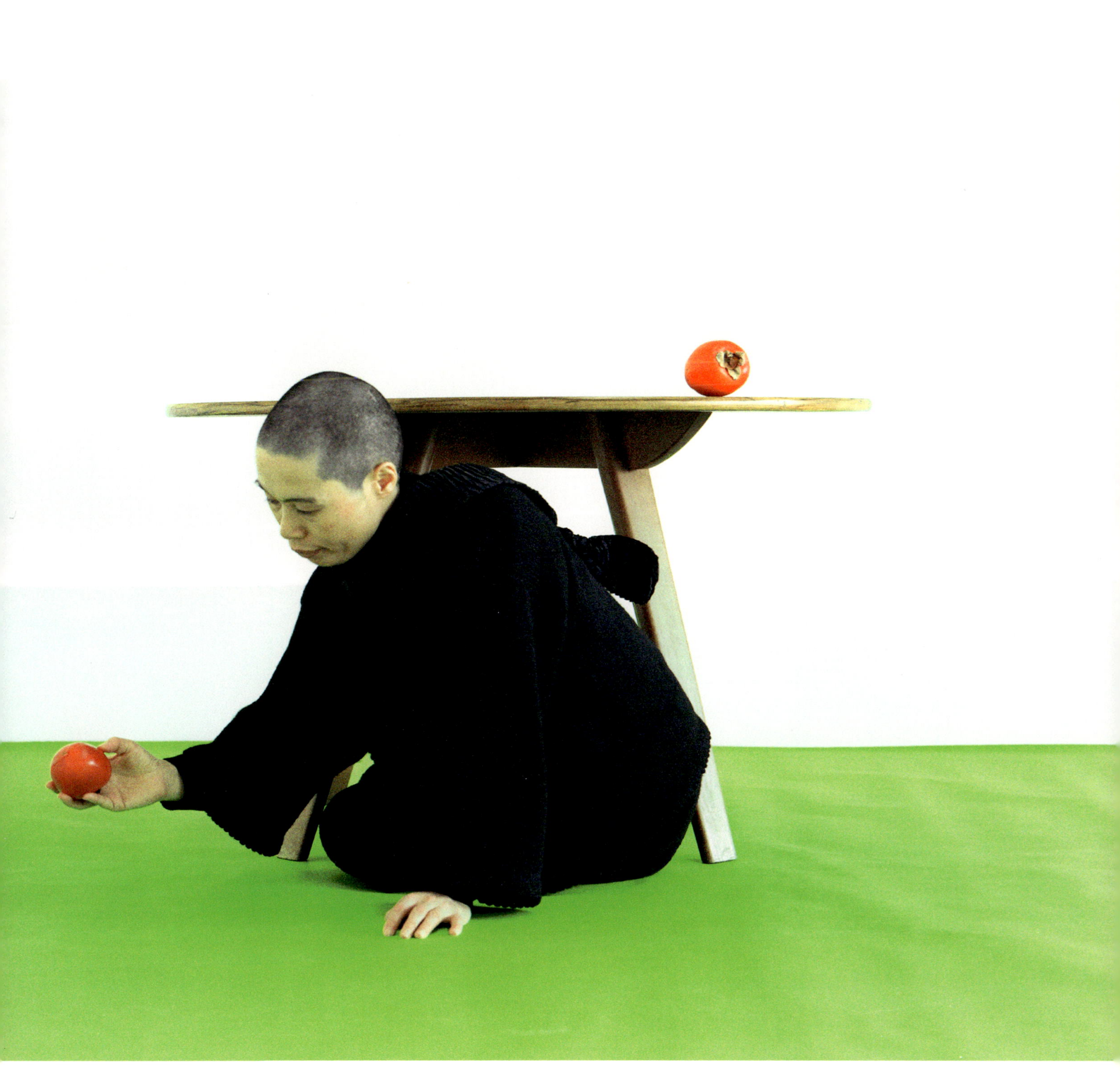

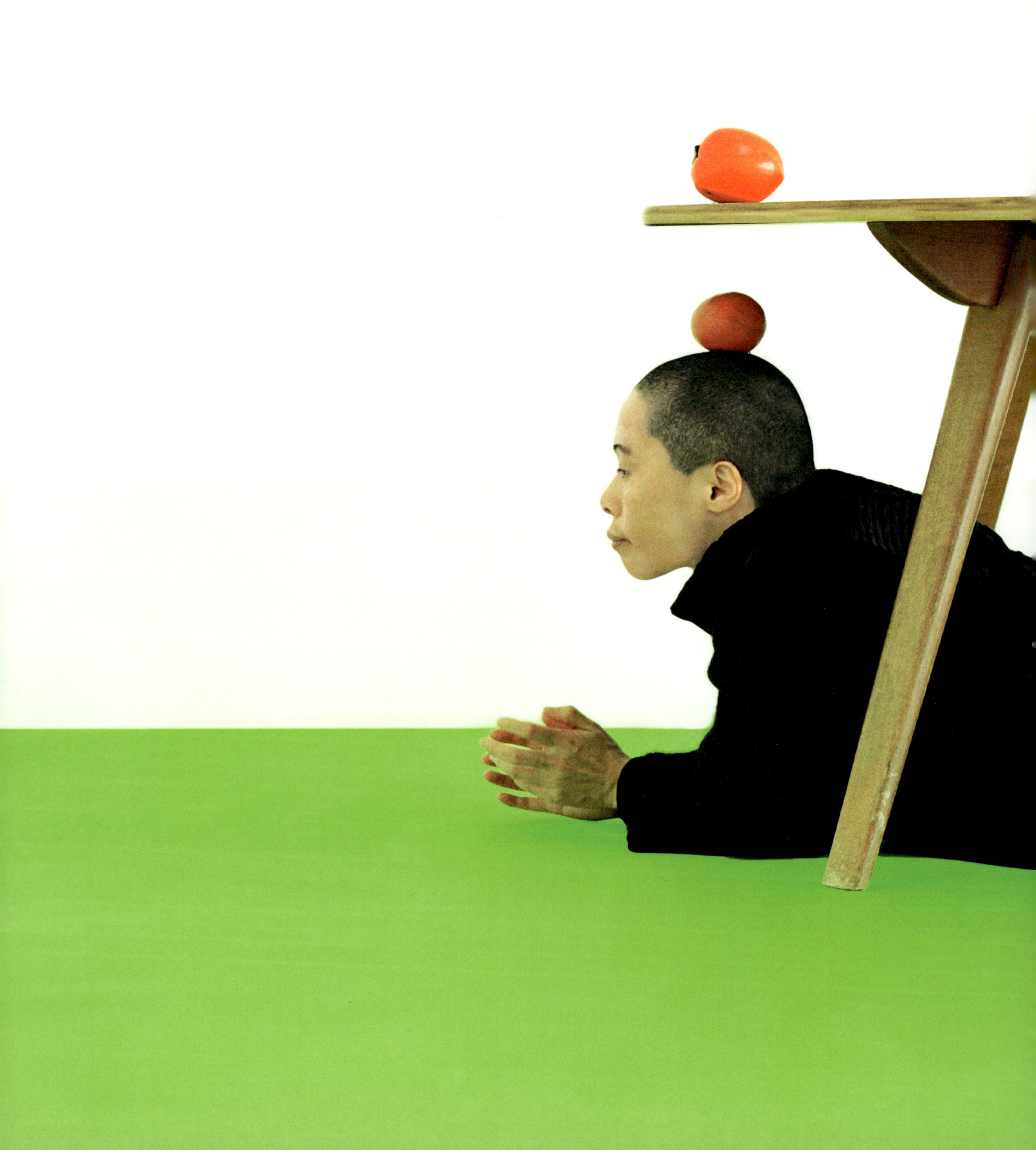

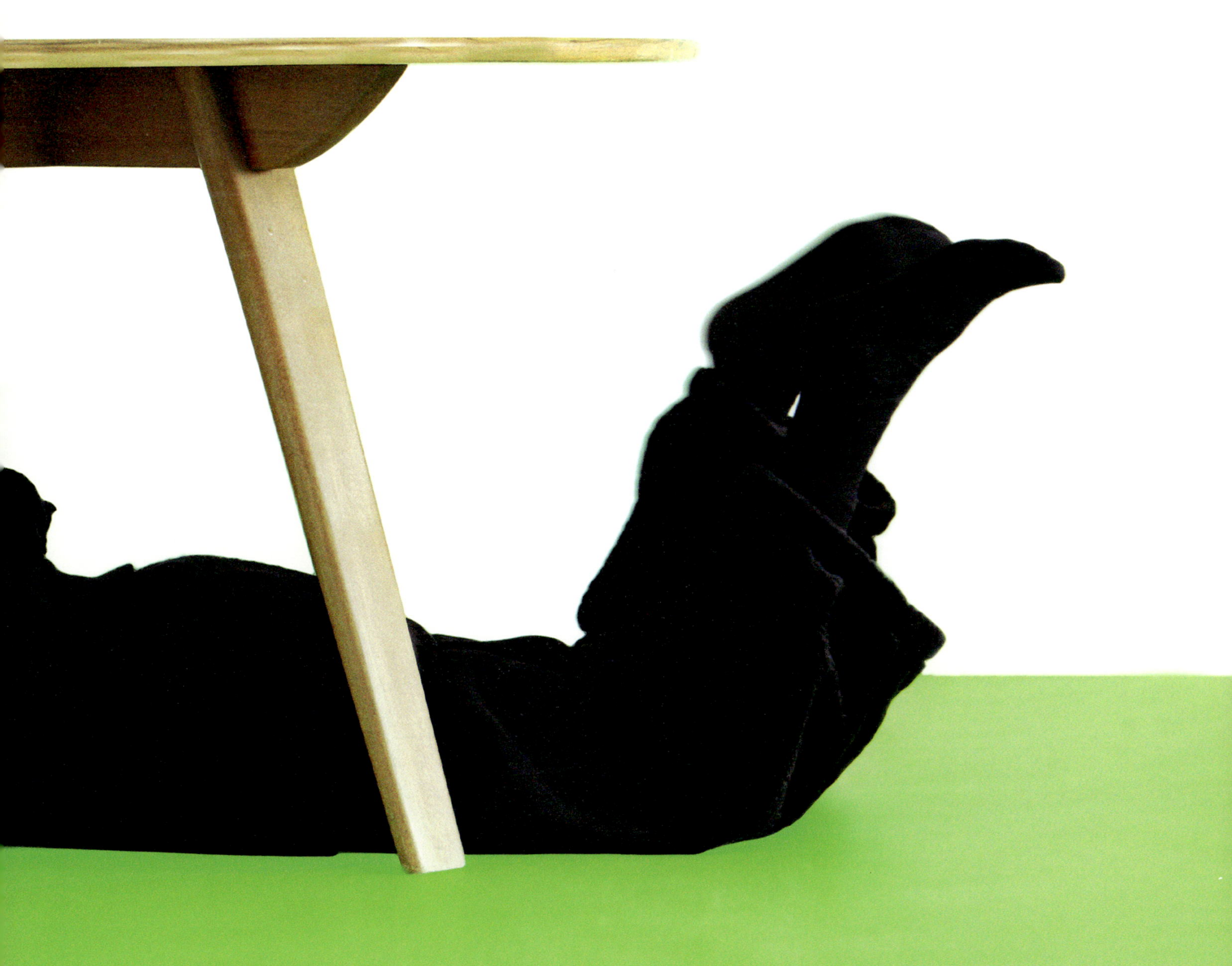

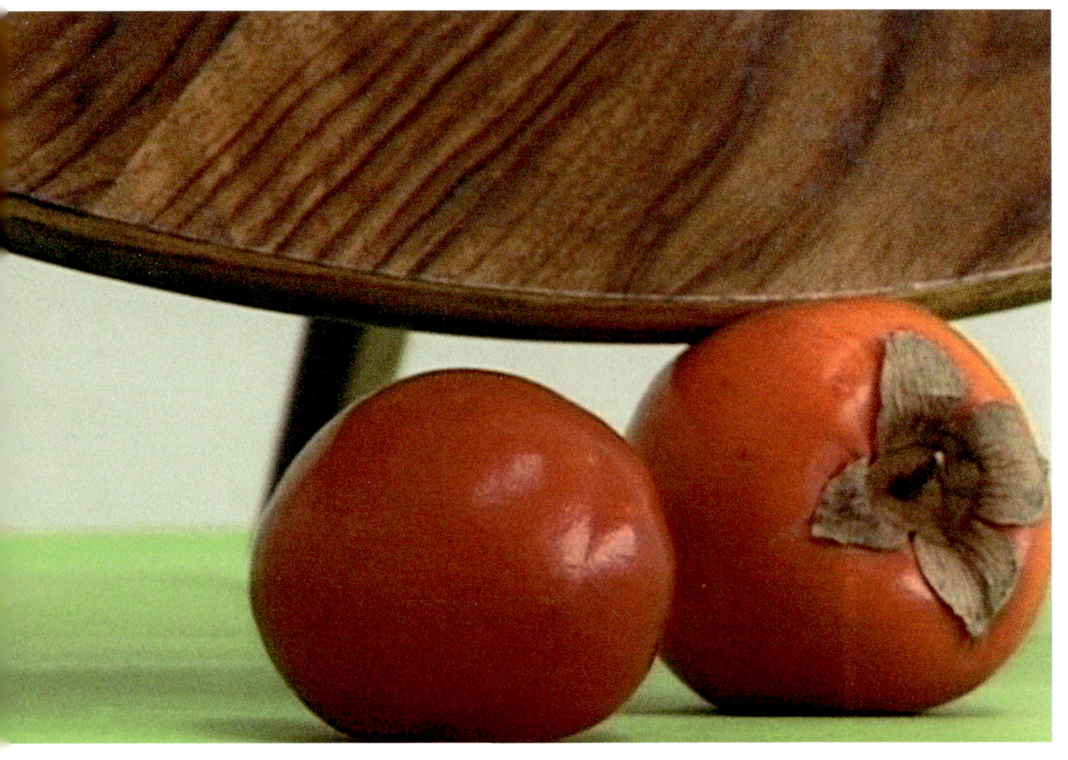

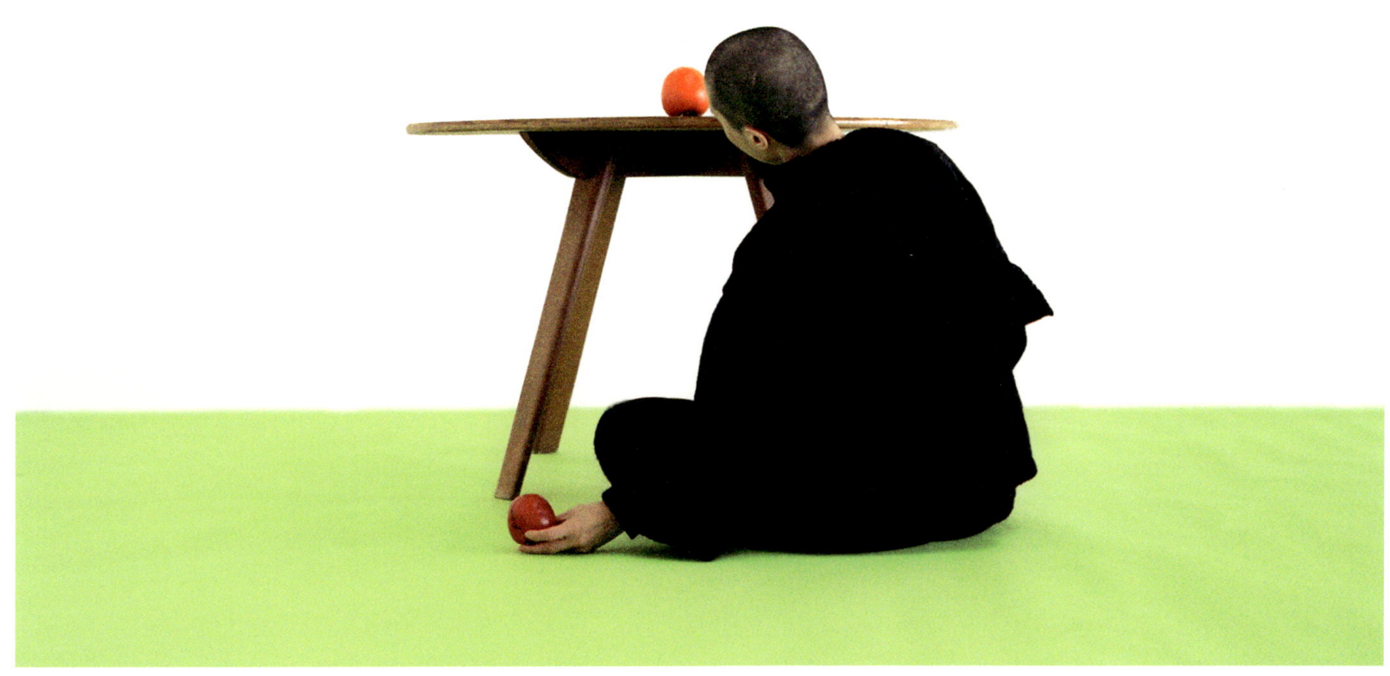

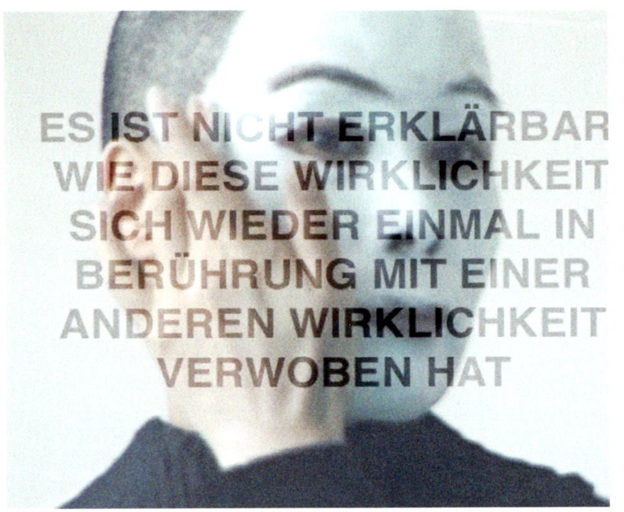

**DU WIRST VON DER
MELODIE BETÖRT,
SOLANGE DU VON IHR
BESEELT BIST**

Schein und Wirklichkeit, Video 2003

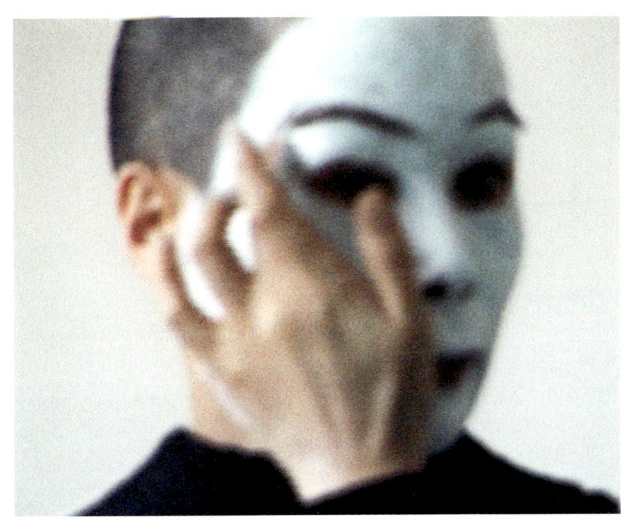

Daniela Zymann

Dislocated Visual Worlds

While viewing the photographic and filmic works by S'nim Oh, the question arises of whether it is possible to represent the self in a culture marked by migration, fragmentation, and hyrbridity. The self at disposition here is not the autobiographical self, which maneuvers between truth and fiction, author and subject, and is defined by a unified, hermetic, and therefore universalist set of regulations governing representation. S'nim Oh's works show that the task of elaborating upon the depiction of the type of subject that has abandoned any sort of outdated, hollow notion of homogeneity is one of the challenges facing contemporary artists.

Putting identity into the game means more than putting the self into the image. Of perforce, it also touches upon the problems inherent in representation and communication. It involves the issue of »the essence« or »the site« of culture. How is it possible to re-appropriate and reformulate the traditional hegemony of western modes of representation and its formalized set of rules, without turning the newly acquired territory into a pure genre? What kinds of figures of thought and representation do artists like S'nim Oh use in order to create complex visual forms that (also) treat the issue of cultural difference as a productive disorientation, not as the establishment of a kind of difference that can be occupied?

Following the interpretation of Homi Bhabhas and others, I would like to define the kind of cultural difference addressed here as a kind of intersection and overlap of those aspects that determine identity today. That means defining it through divergent memberships in cultural, class-, site-, and gender-specific, symbolic amalgamations, not as an ethnic position – here, meaning S'nim Oh's Korean origins. Questioning individualization as a result of cultural difference and »dis-location« conceals the possibilities posed by a narrative potential, which American-Korean theorist Miwon Kwon describes as follows in her article »Imagining an Impossible World Picture.« »It may be more comforting to perceive and/or imagine oneself in relation to a cohesive whole, be it a city or a more abstract social structure. But it seems to me that individual self-recognition, which is the fundamental basis for the possibilities of a collective formation, is not a continuous state of consciousness, but rather a scattered, messy desire based on infrequent and unpredictable moments of epiphanous realizations of one's subjectivity. It is not through a continuous accumulation of partial mental pictures or memories of familiar spaces/social realities that one consolidates or grounds one's sense of place/self. Instead, it is through the very shock of ruptures, incongruencies, and discontinuities that one is reminded (in negation) of the sense of wholeness and place. For me, it was precisely at the moment of recognizing my own erasure that I imagined myself as a social subject within an impossible world picture.« [1]

The interesting thing about Kwon's description and her other theoretical formation, the »condition of ungrounded transience«, is the idea that identity can be narrated and depicted as increasingly divided from a fixed understanding of place, homeland, and self. This severance is, however, also marked by a sense of connection and loss, as well as by the necessity of having to portray what has been lost as something that cannot be retrieved. I would like to ascribe porosity and impermanence, as well as the feeling of connection and the way it is processed to S'nim Oh's works. »My World is unsayable«, »Shine and Reality«, or »Wishes« refer to an inarticulateness that unite equal measures of doubling (shine/reality – world/inexpressible – wish) and references to reality (world/reality).

S'nim Oh uses imaginary dislocating and locating in ways that conceal the possibility of constantly refiguring the process. This happens primarily in the territory of the self, meaning on the surface of a performative, transforming self-image that lies beyond the traditionally familiar. The persona S'nim Oh depicts is marked by the kind of ambivalence that uses doubling, reproductions, and differences to explode the notion of belonging to a homelike, familiar image of the world. This doubling, however, should not be interpreted as a boundary drawn between the inside and outside, between the self and non-space, since the intervention and invention displayed by the hybrid subject includes equal amounts of interior and exterior. S'nim Oh's depictions and self-portraits seem to not only comprehend inside and outside equally, but also suggest visual worlds, undepicted aspects of the past, of the imagined past, moments that do not belong to the dispositive of the »grand narratives«, but haunt the present and search for figuration.

For me, the genuinely key concept in this context is »artificiality«, in the sense of imagination, alienation, fragmentation, doubling, and aporia. S'nim Oh photographic and filmic works employ the concept of artificiality – »staged images«, carefully composed scenographic images that stage »hybrid moments« in terms of gesture, attitude, expression, color composition, and clothing. Yet this artificiality should not be regarded as the opposite of »reality«. Reality can be shaped through description, design, and re-arrangement. Reality is never neutral, but is constantly being re-negotiated. »The terms ›alienation‹ and ›reflexivity‹ are no longer simply distancing techniques, as long as the separation between the ›textual artistic gesture‹ and ›social attitude‹ is maintained.« To follow Trinh T. Minh-Ha's train of thought, the concept of »elsewhere within here«[2] can be used in this context. The simultaneity of »here and now«, of »letting go«, and »elsewhere« very aptly expresses the interim state describing the topography of S'nim Oh's works in terms of place, psyche, gender-specificity, and art.

»Elsewhere within here«[2] also opens up access to the imaginary, meaning, to that space that is never completely covered by any sort of history. It exists in between. The imaginary is the »order« of the unarticulated aspect of the psyche. It describes the relationship between the self and its (unconscious) images. This imaginary space not only refers to individual fantasies from the subconscious of individuals, but there are associations with the symbolic order, an order that is part of the collective.

S'nim Oh delineates »Elsewhere« as »Wishes« – which, however, should not be construed as »fiction«, as described elsewhere, but perhaps understood in Ludwig Wittgenstein's sense of HYPERLINK »http://de.wikipedia.org/wiki/Ludwig_Wittgenstein« a characteristic experience, such as to recognize, to remember. The wishes S'nim Oh describes are elsewhere, in between, perhaps between west/east, male/female, here/there, inside/outside, language/behavior, artificiality/reality, memory/loss, tradition/appropriation, transformation/
legacy. It is the constant doubling of all values that forms the conceptual horizon of S'nim Oh's artistic practice, which then challenges us to reconsider issues of representation and difference in a productive manner.

»Because when you talk about difference, there are many ways to receive it; if one simply understands it as a division between culture, between people, between entities, one can't go very far with it. But when that difference between entities is being worked out as a difference also within, things start opening up. Inside and outside are both expanded. Within each entity, there is a vast field and within each self is a multiplicity.«[2]

1 Miwon Kwon, »Imagining an Impossible World Picture«, Lusitania 7 (New York: Lusitania Press, 1995), p. 87.

2 HYPERLINK »http://www.trinhminh-ha.com/« http://www.trinhminh-ha.com/

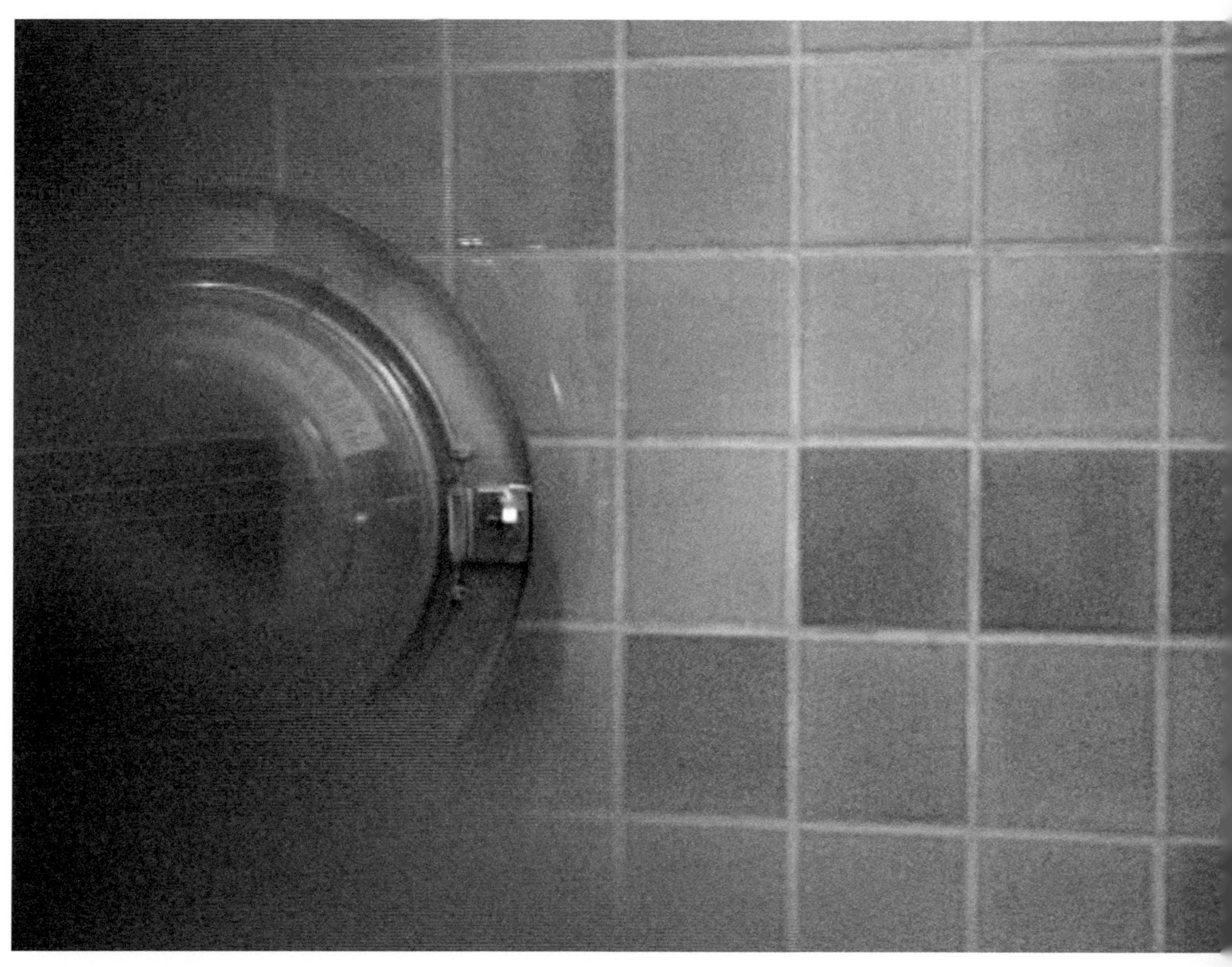

Whenever I am in a good mood, Video 2003

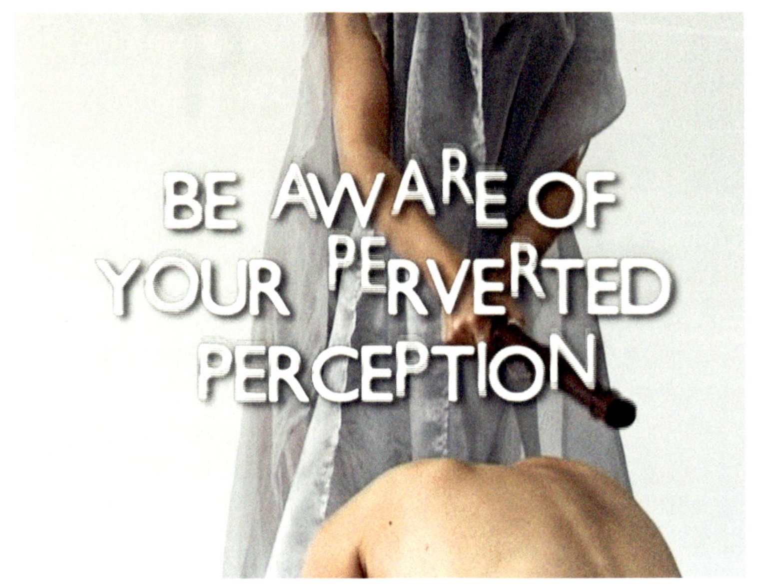

Be aware of your perveted perception, Video 2004

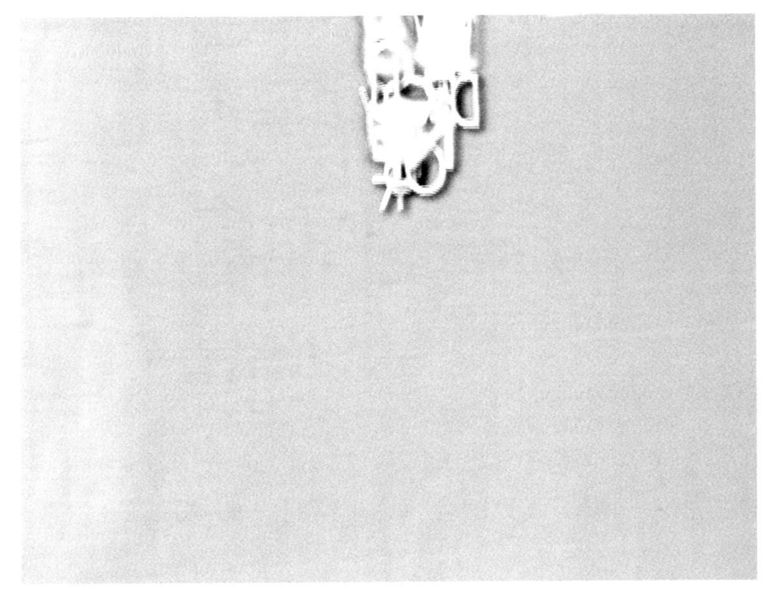

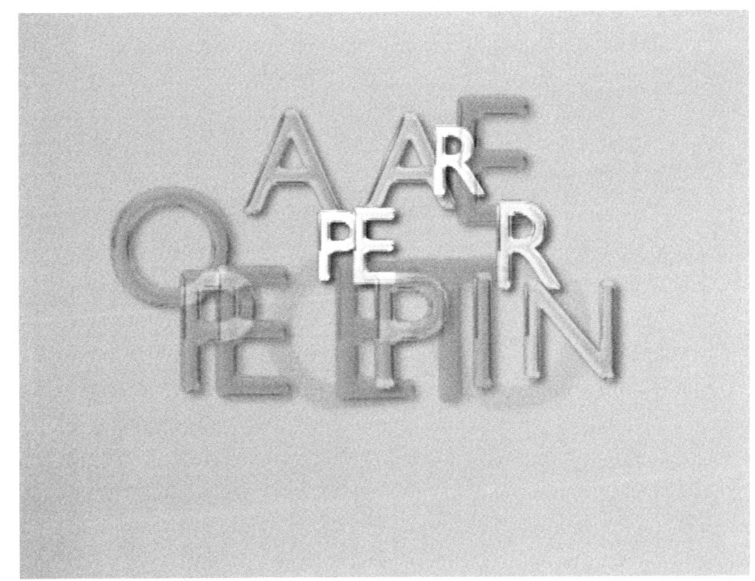

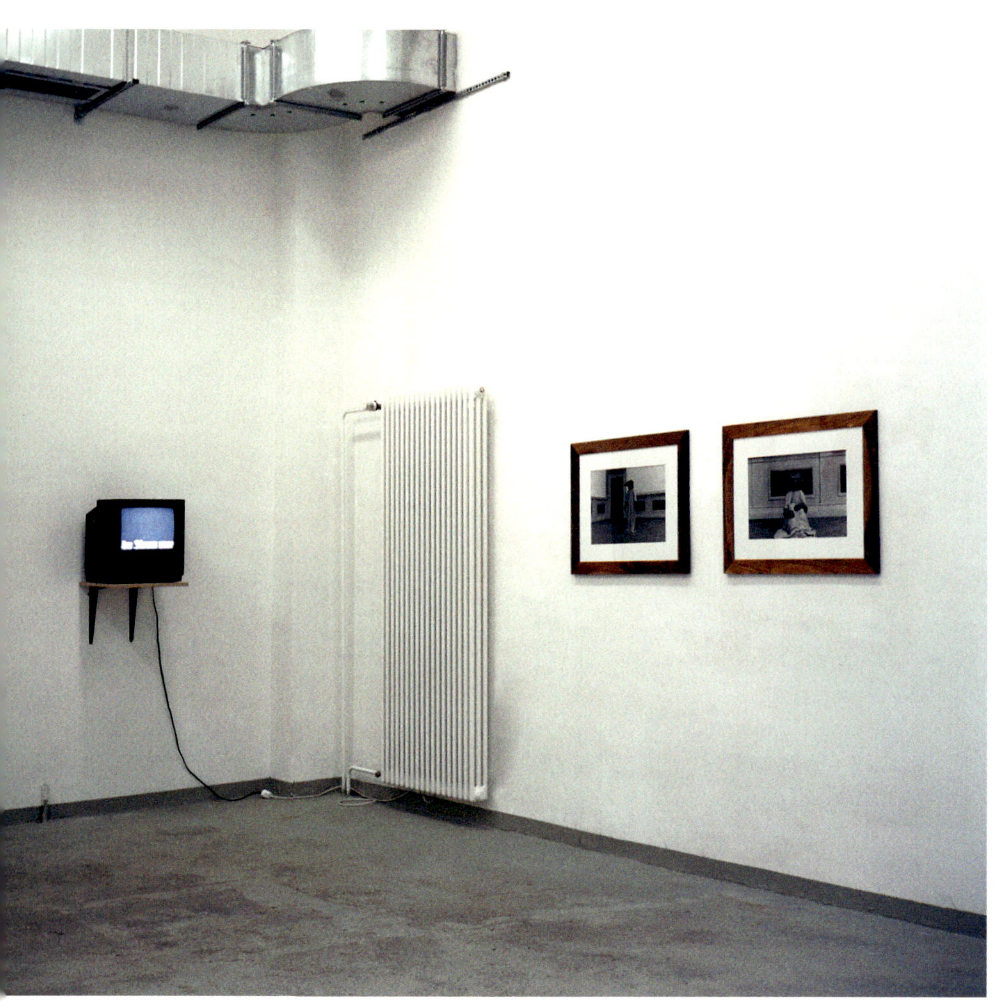

Akademie der Bildenden Künste, München, 2002

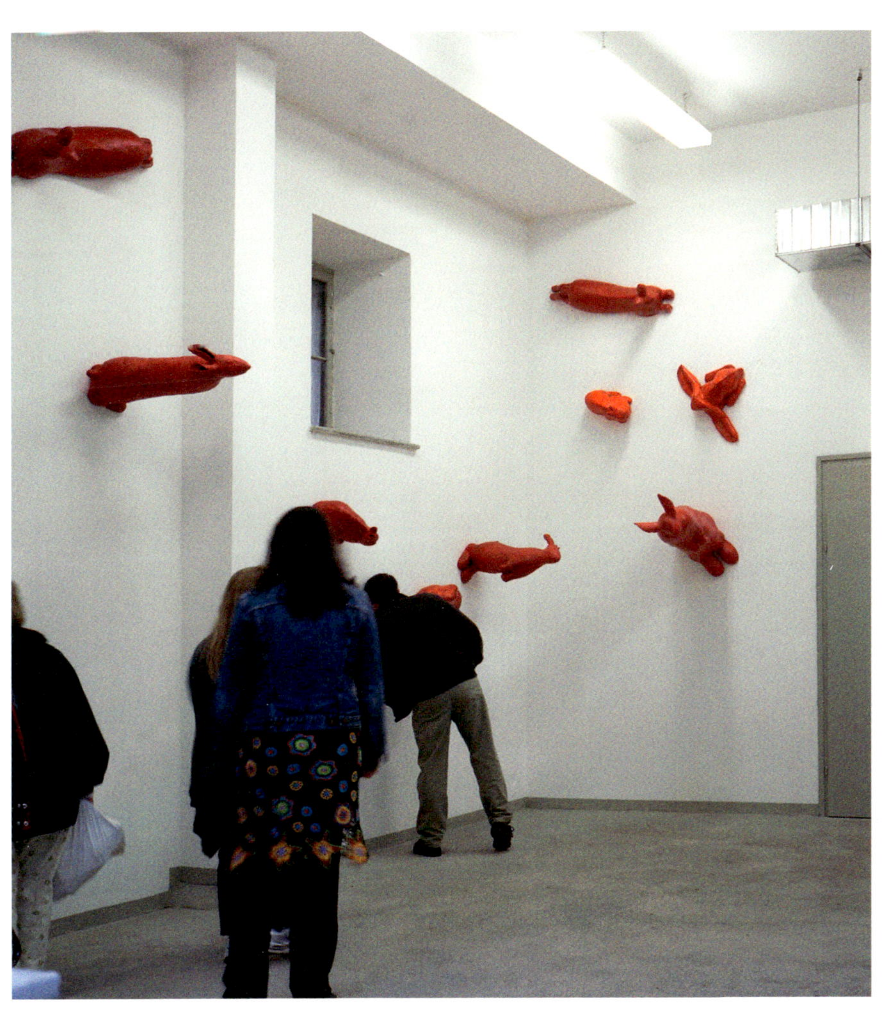

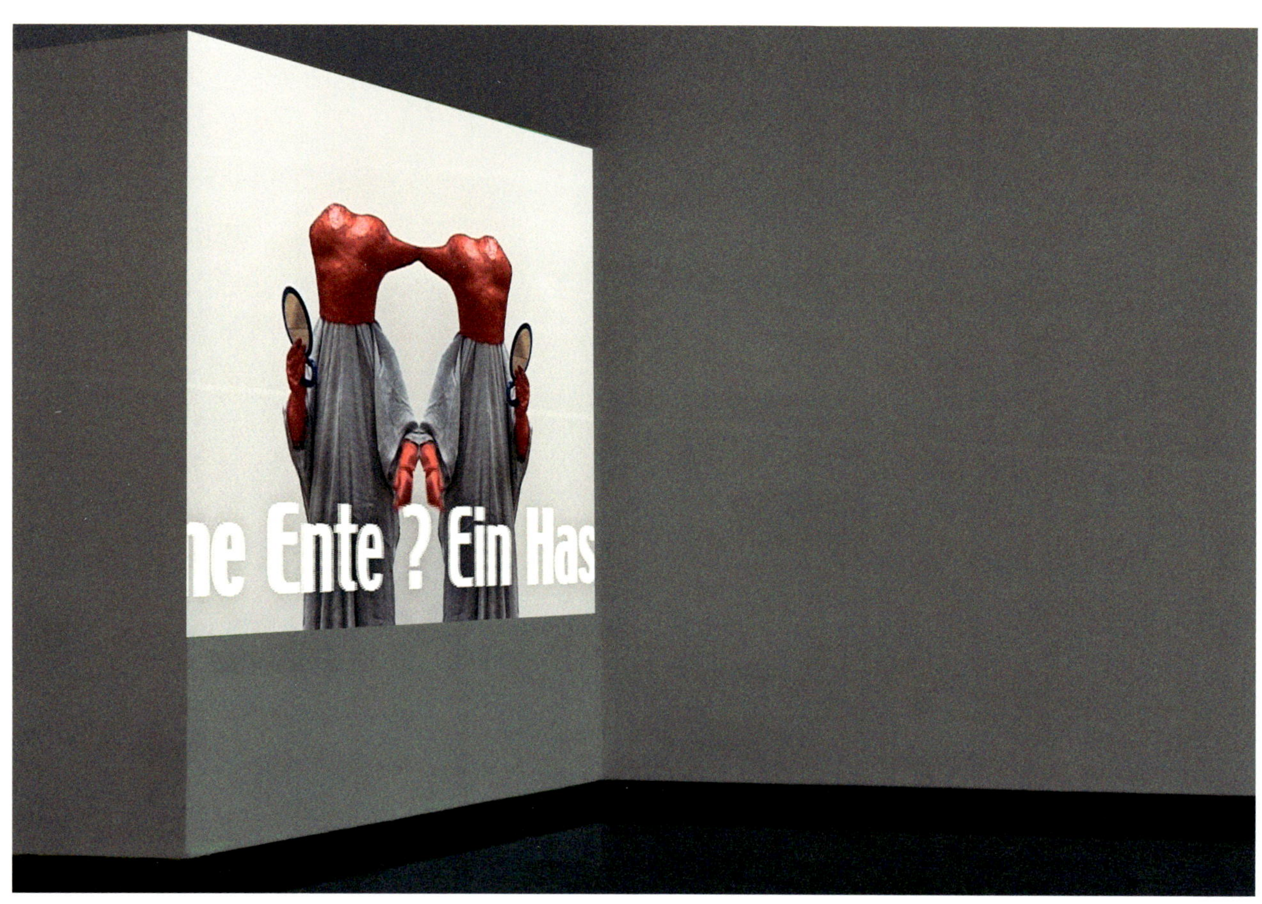

Galerie im Andechshof, Innsbruck, 2002

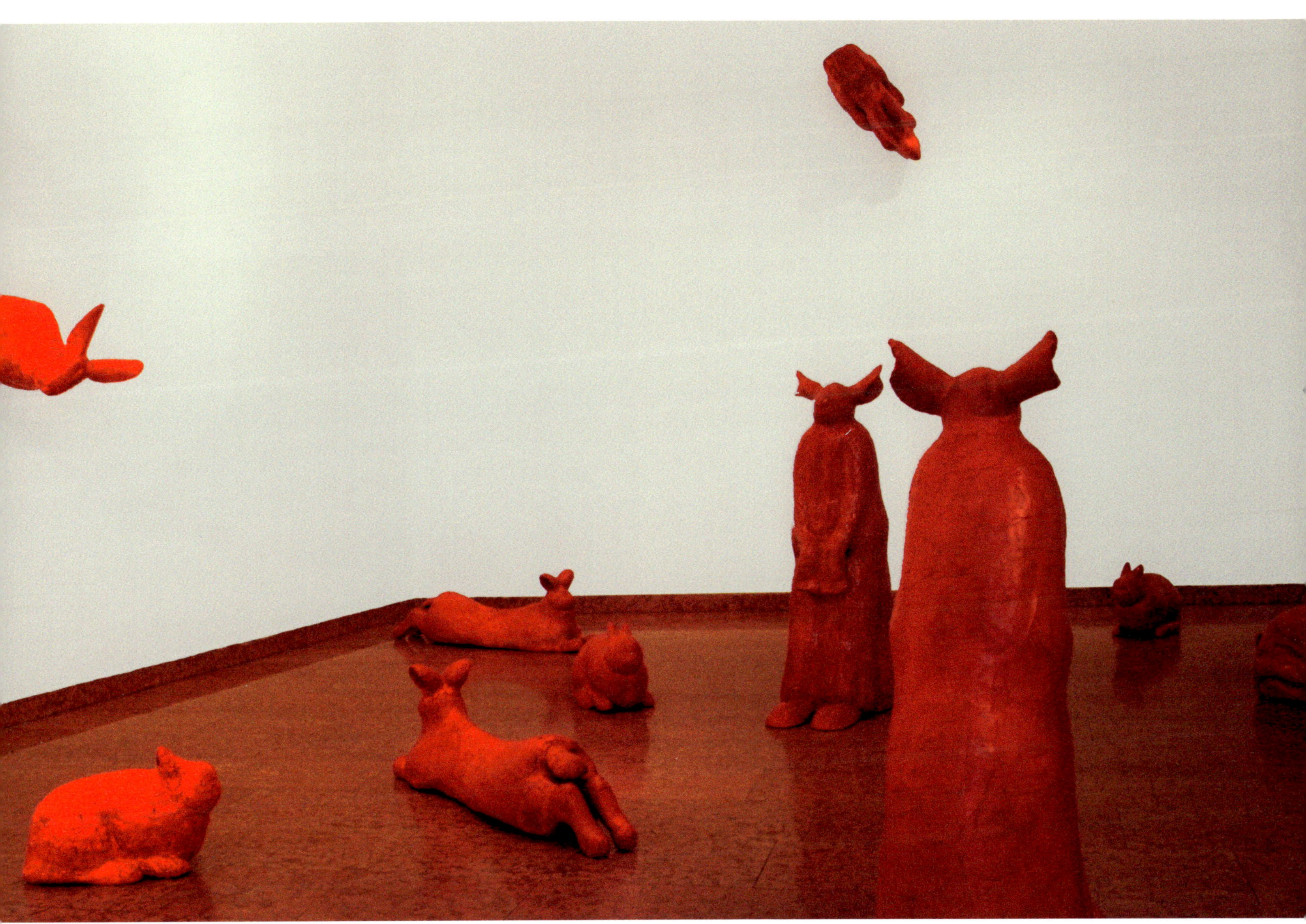

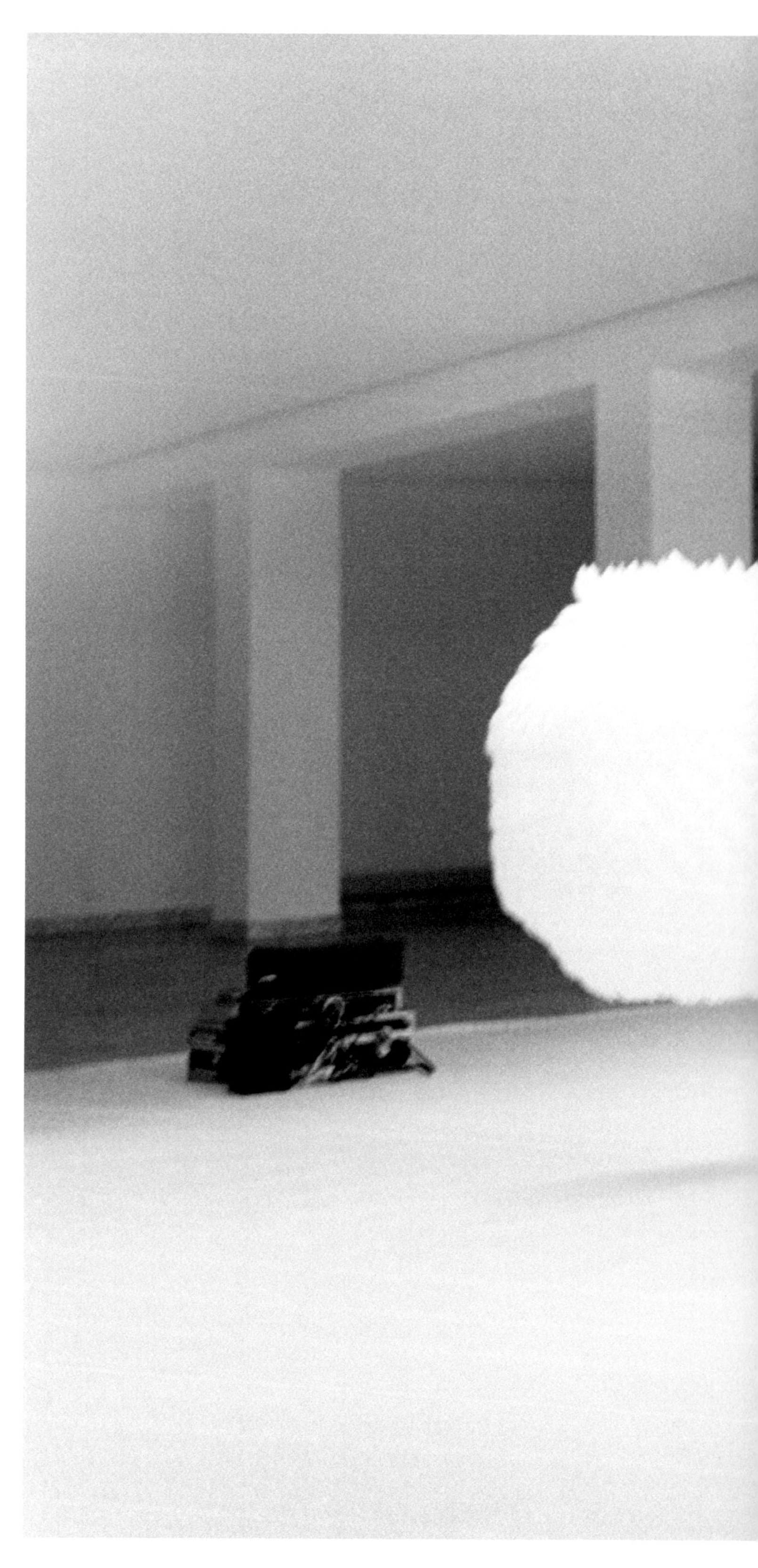

PTS Baden Baden, 2003

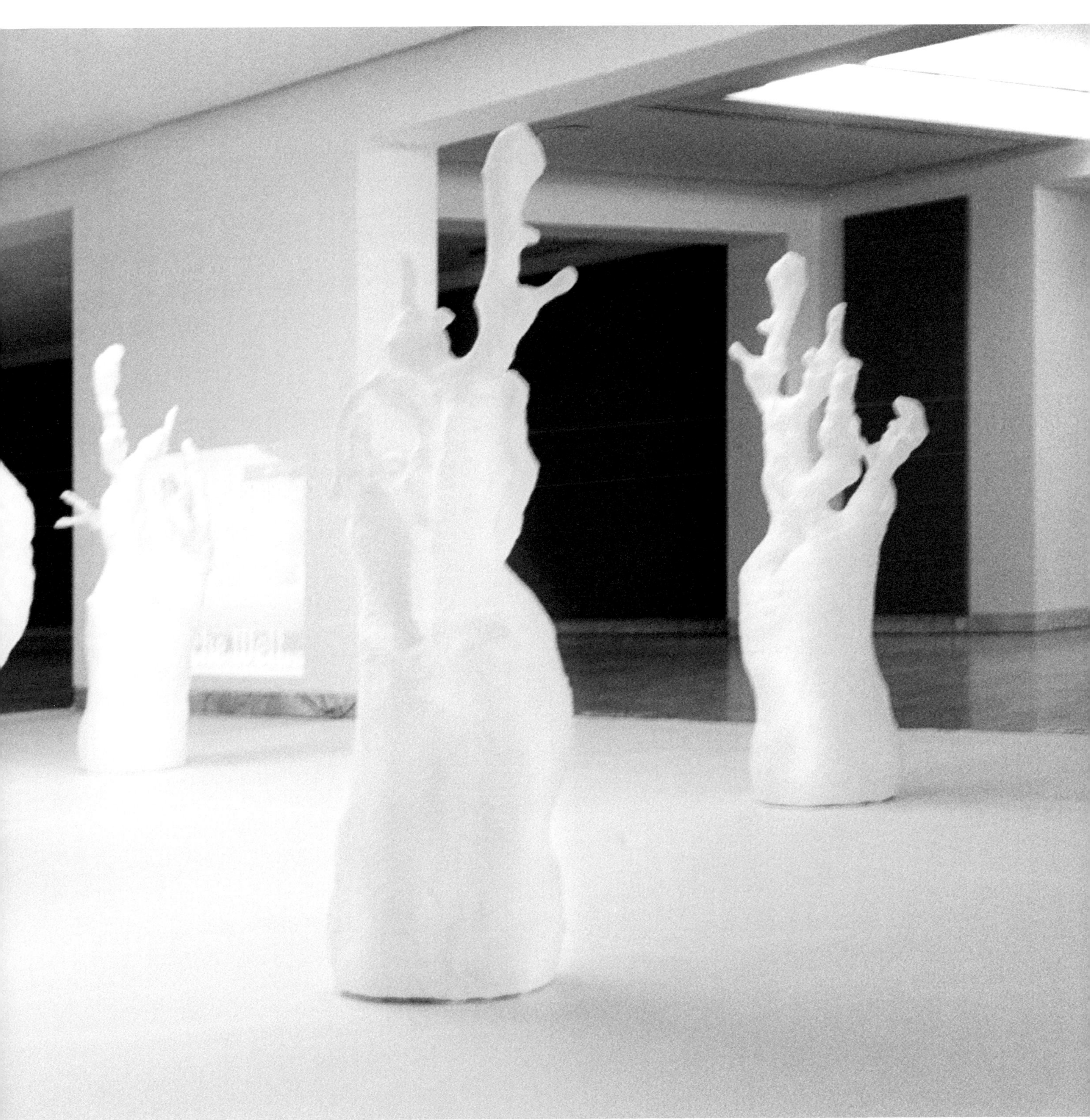

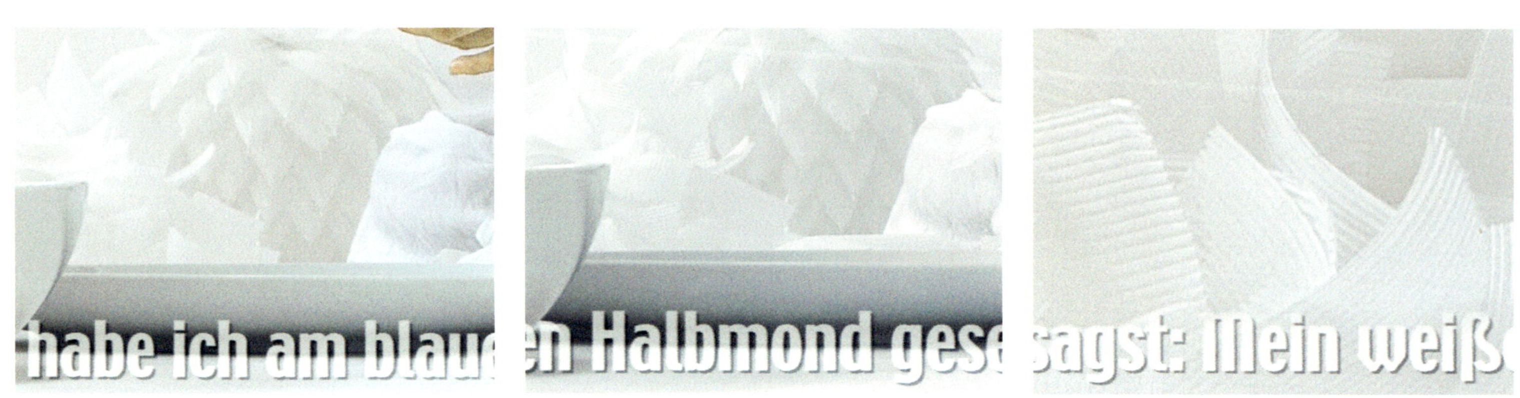

Meine Welt ist unaussprechlich, Video 2003

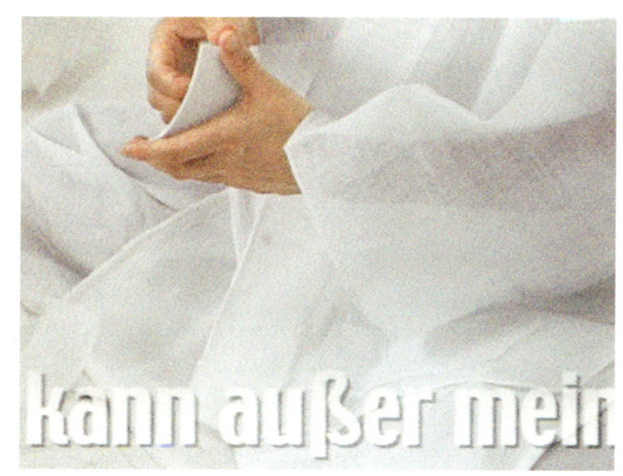
kann außer mein

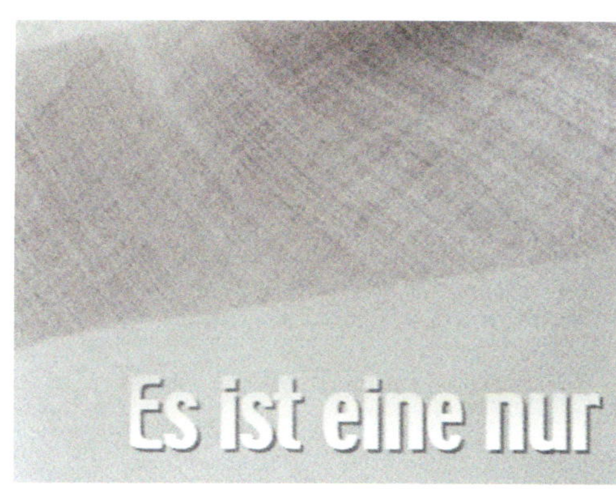
Es ist eine nur

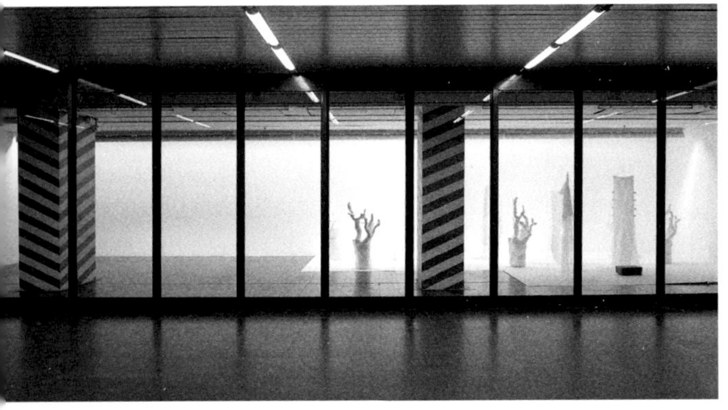

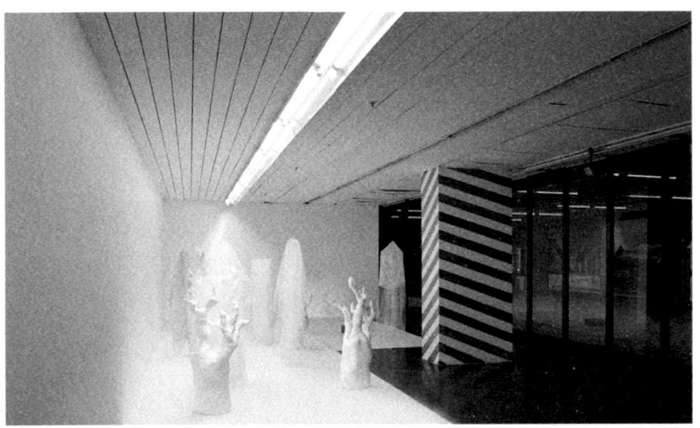

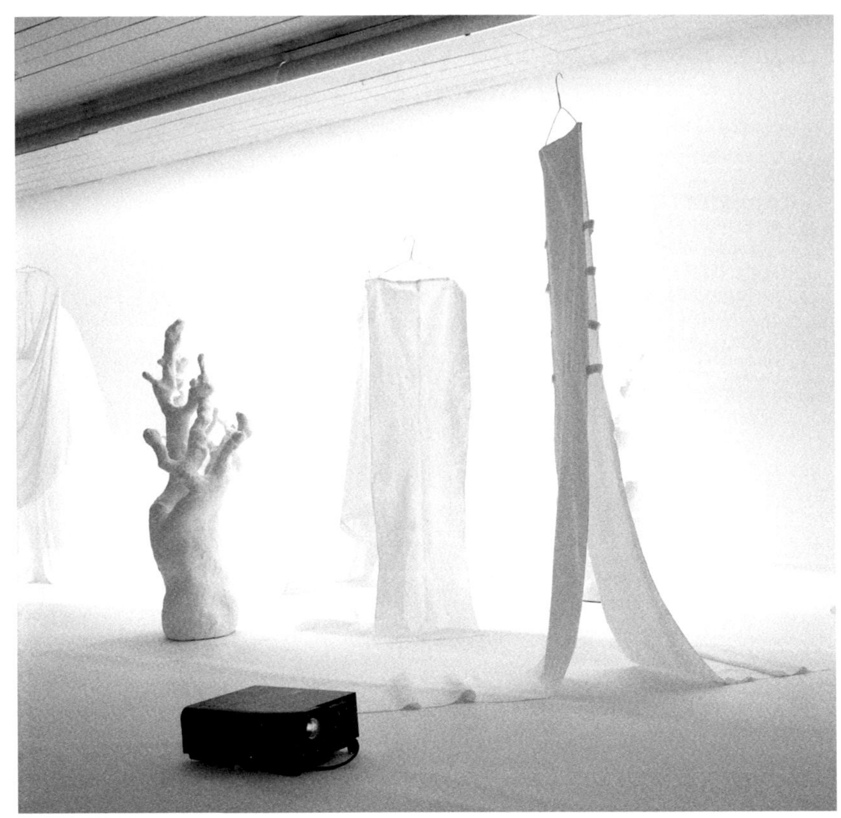

Akademiegalerie, München, 2004

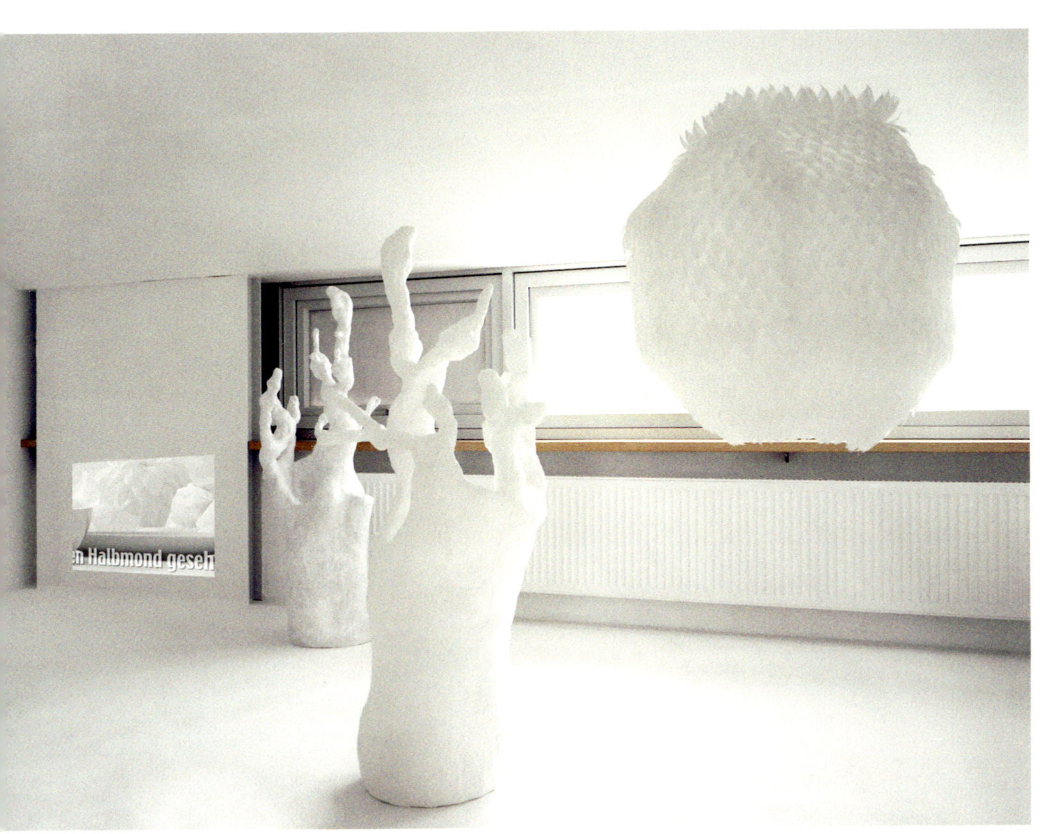

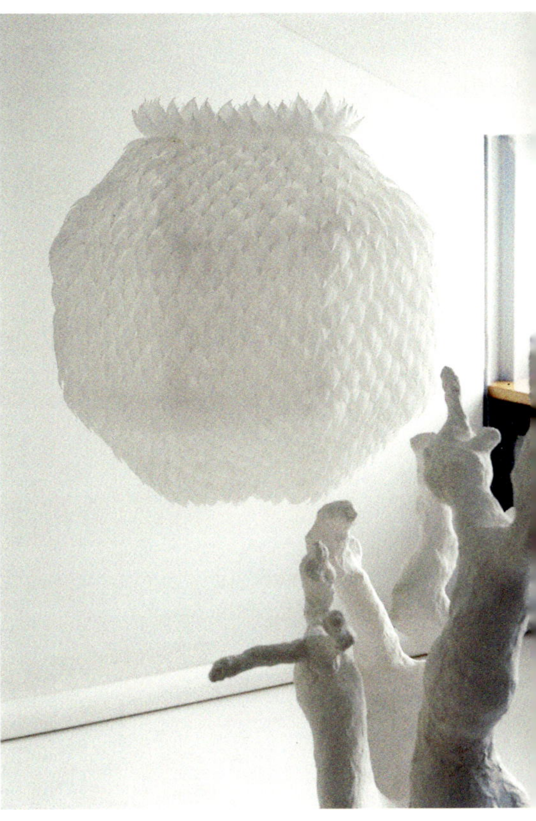

Akademie der Bildenden Künste, München, 2003

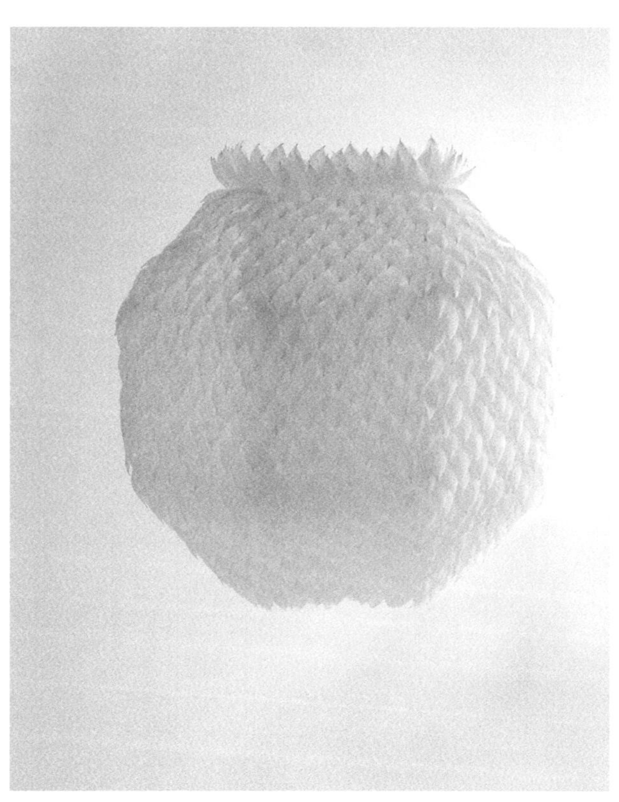

Meine Welt ist unaussprechlich, 2003

Meine Welt ist unaussprechlich, 2003

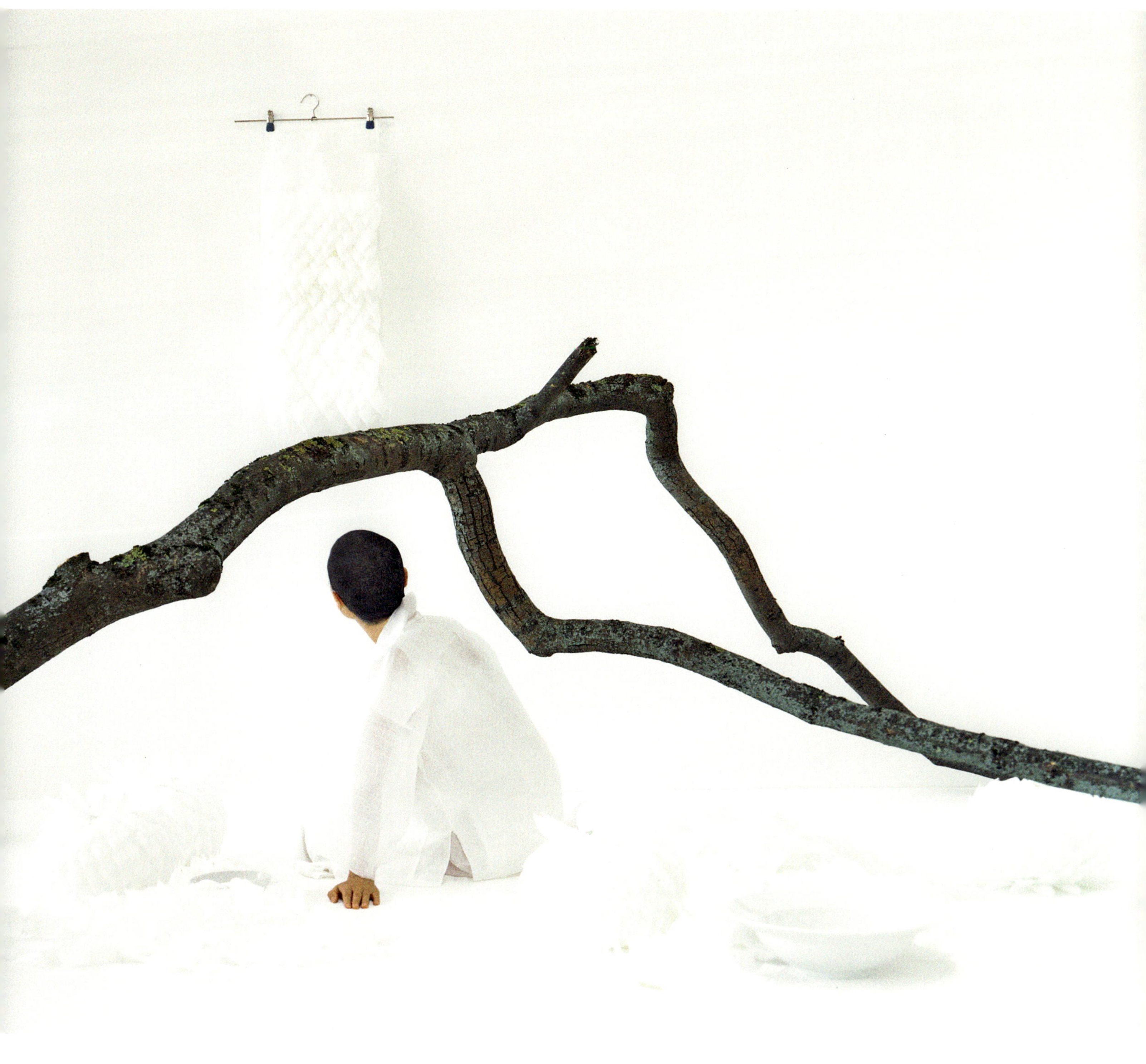

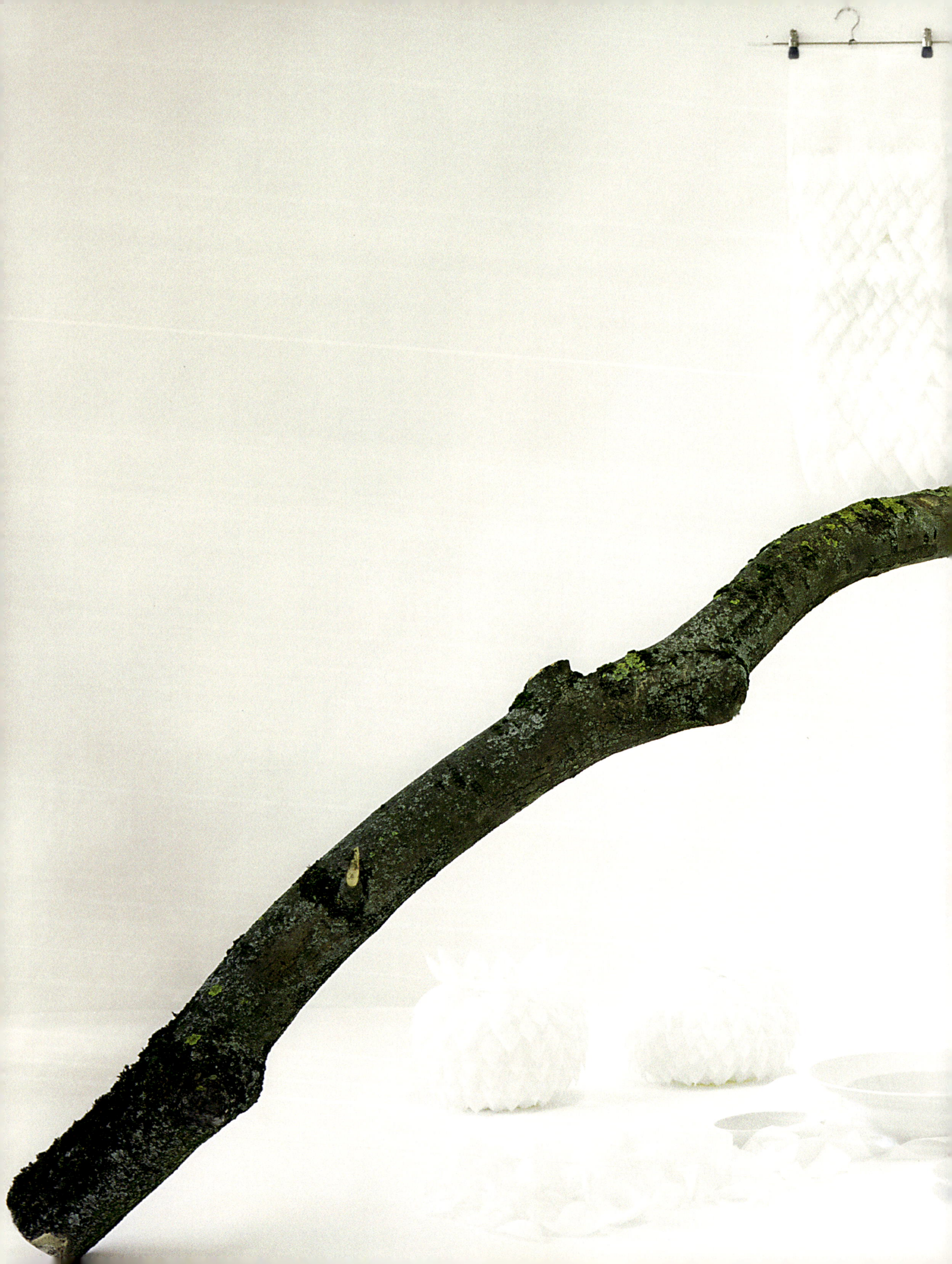

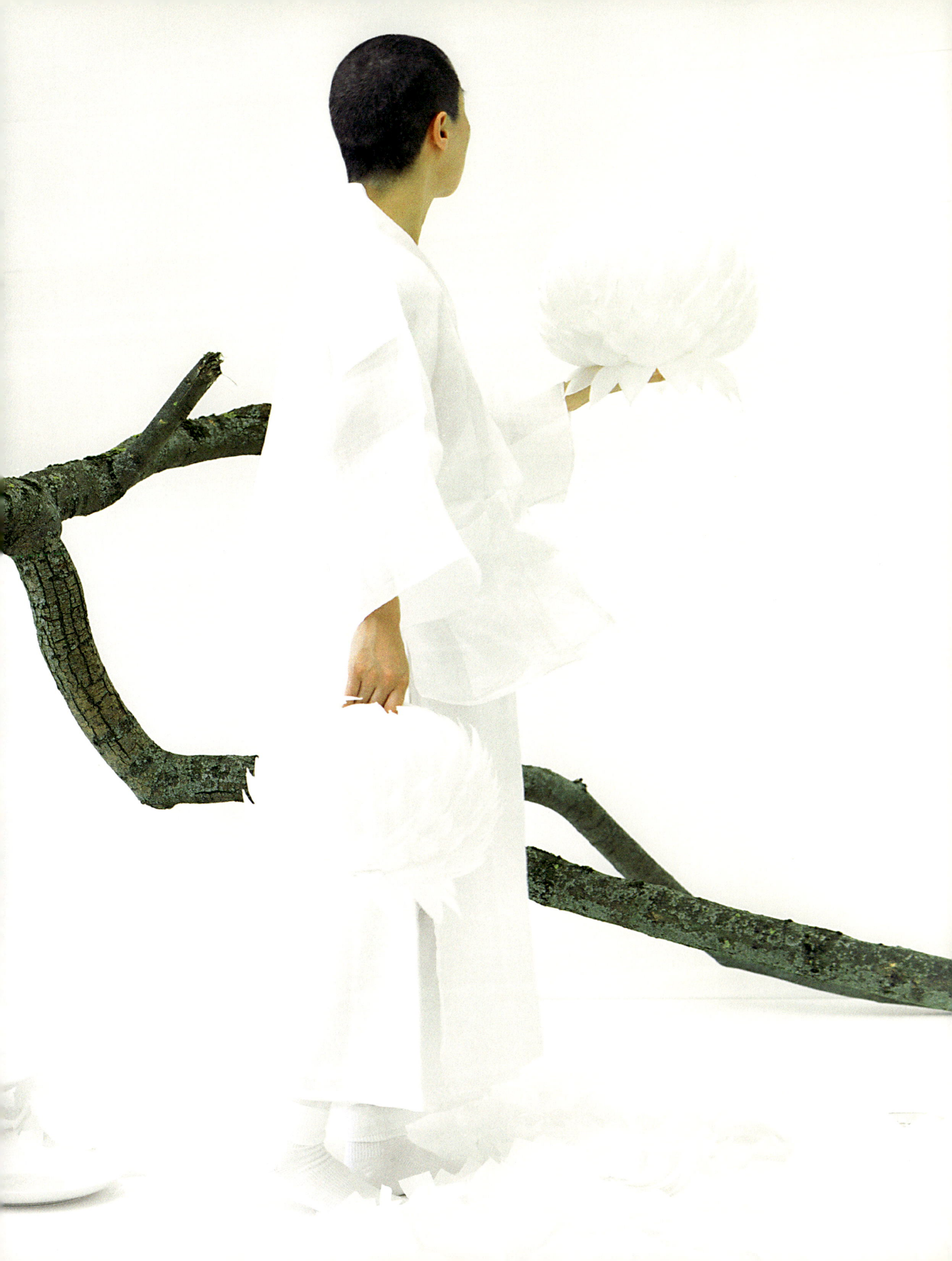

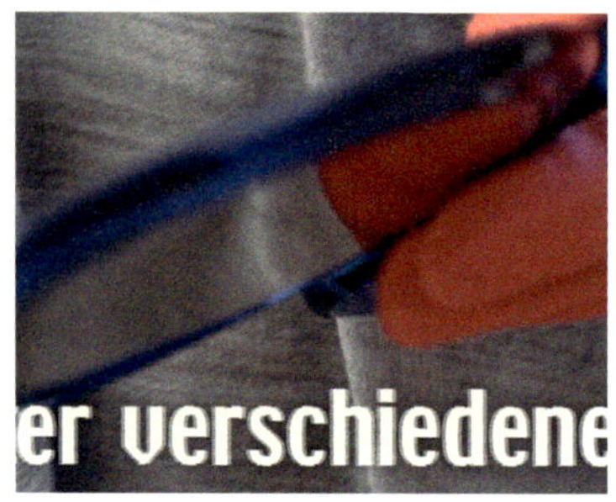

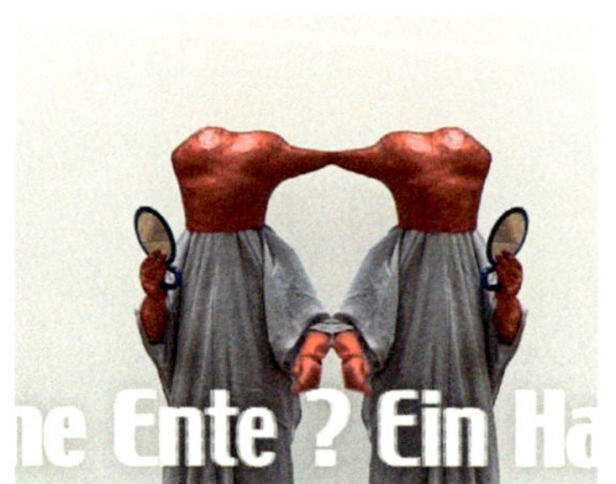

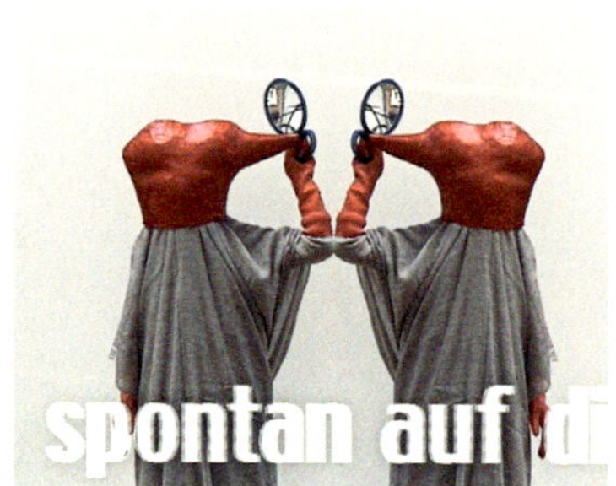

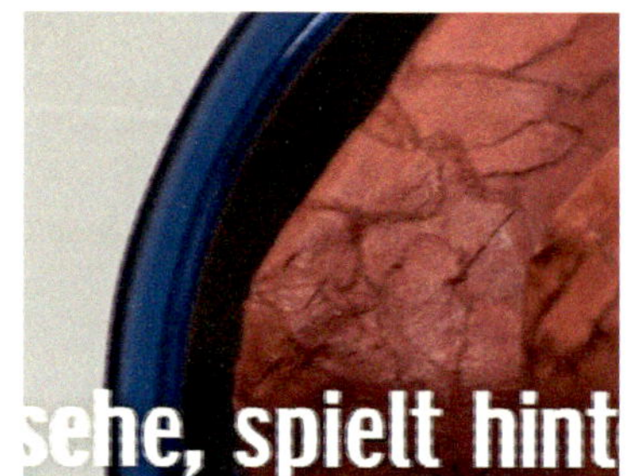

Aspektswechsel, Video 2002

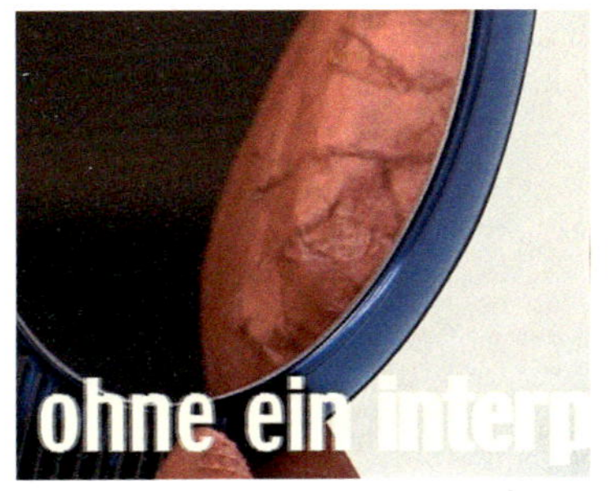
ohne ein

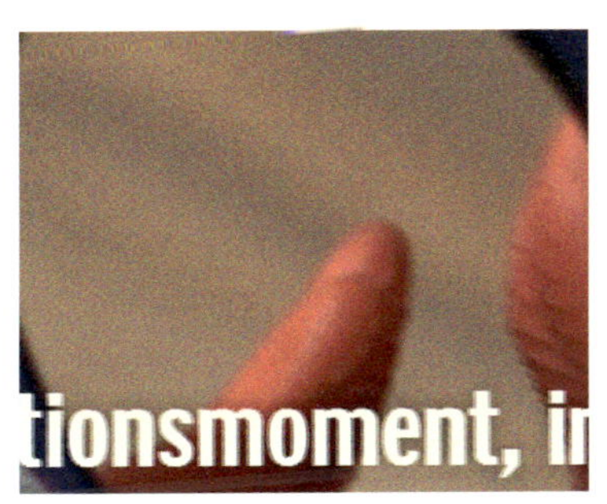
tionsmoment,

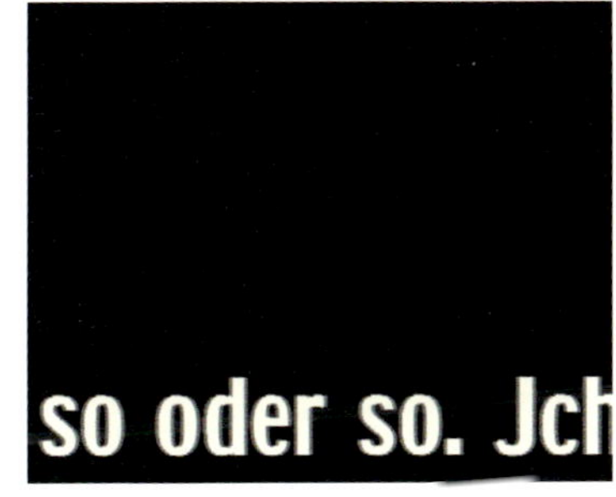
so oder so. Jch

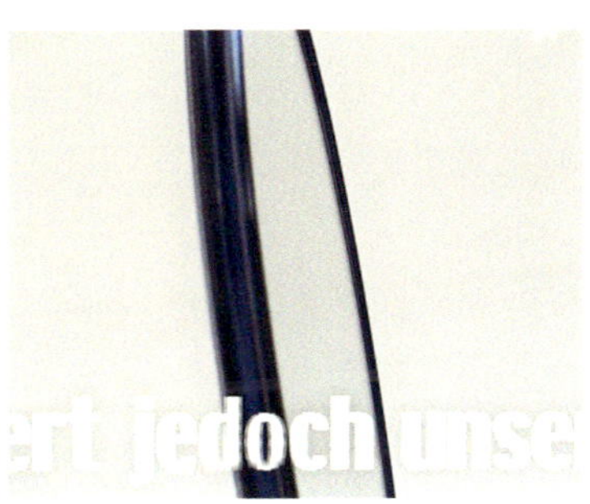

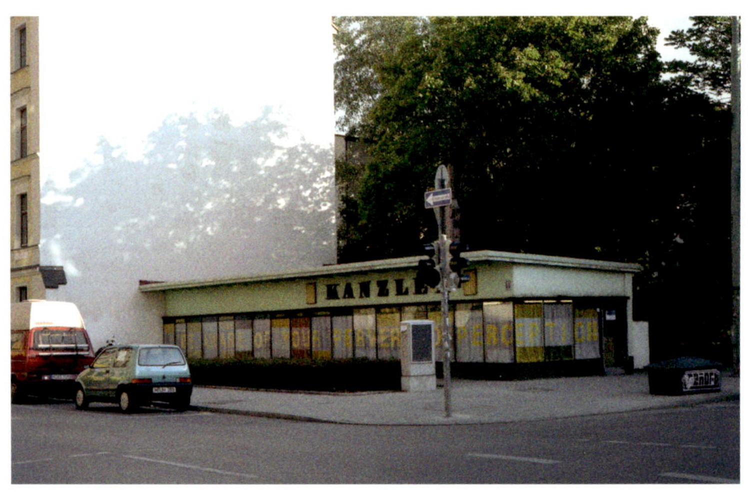

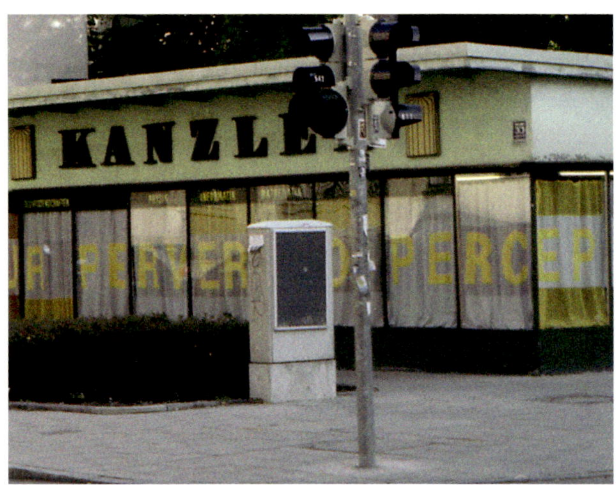

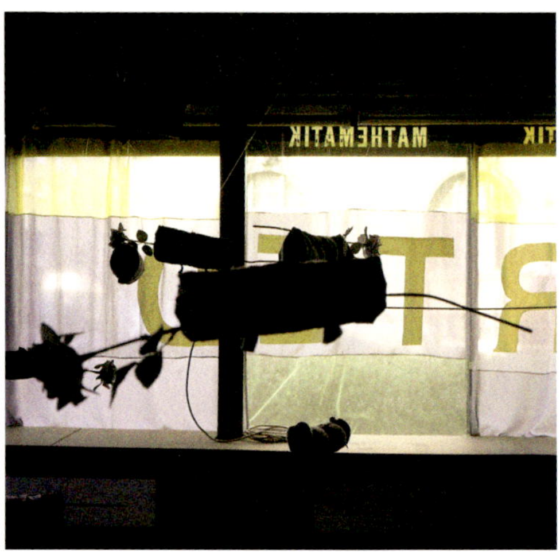

Open Art, Wandergalerie im Kanzler, München, , 2003

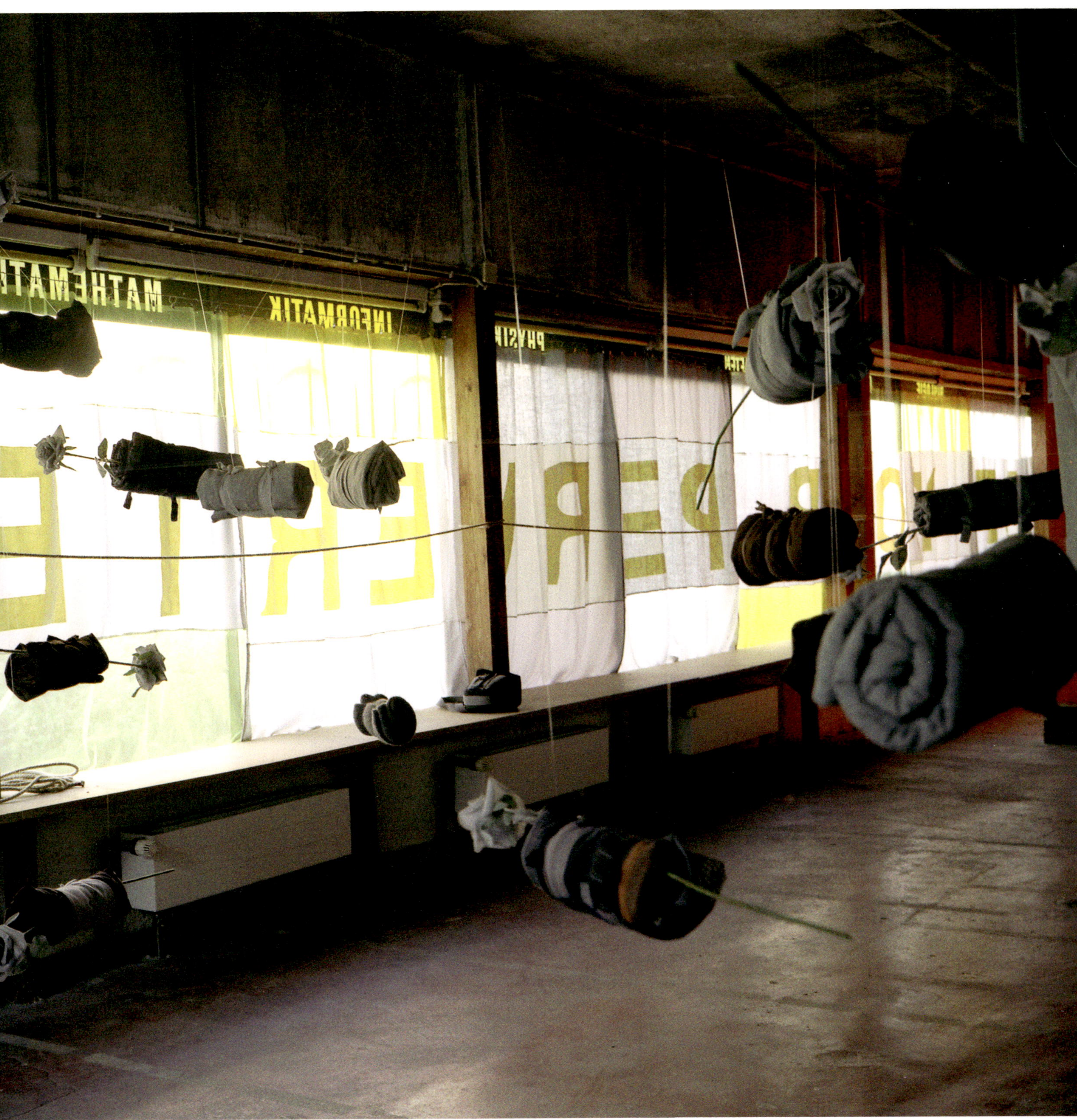
INFORMATIK

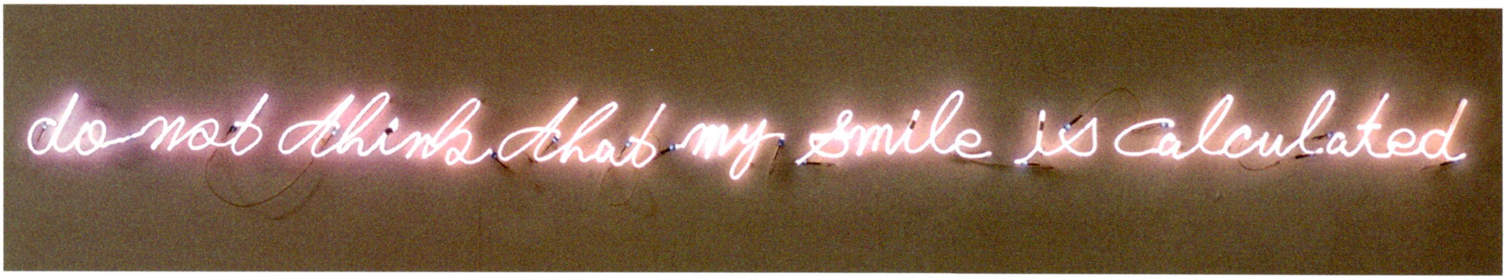

do not think that my smile is calculated

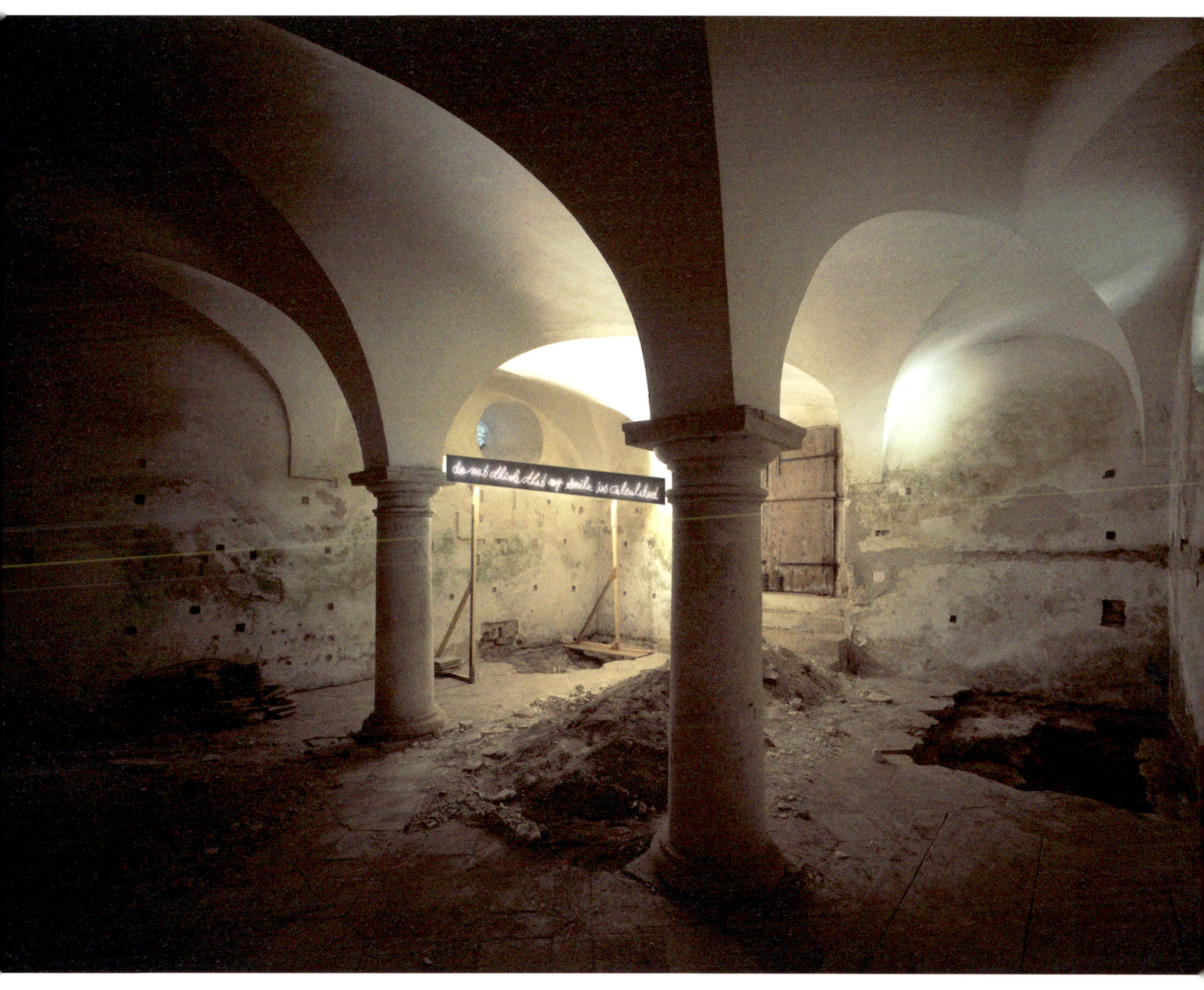

Do not think that my smile is calculated, Kloster Weltenburg, 2005

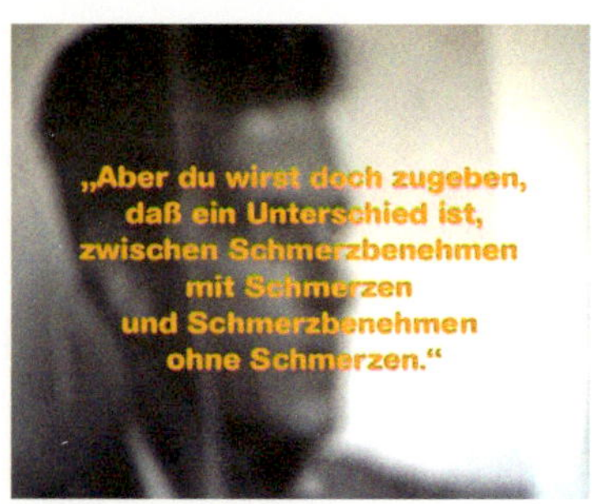

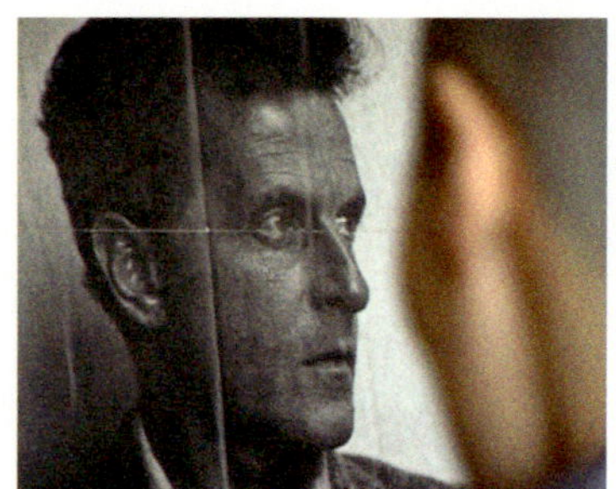

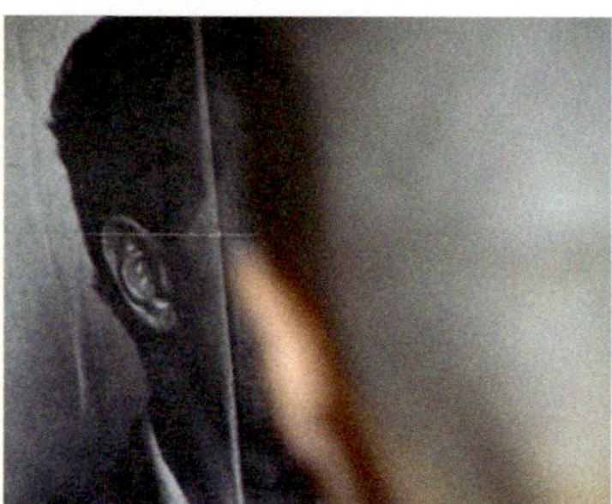

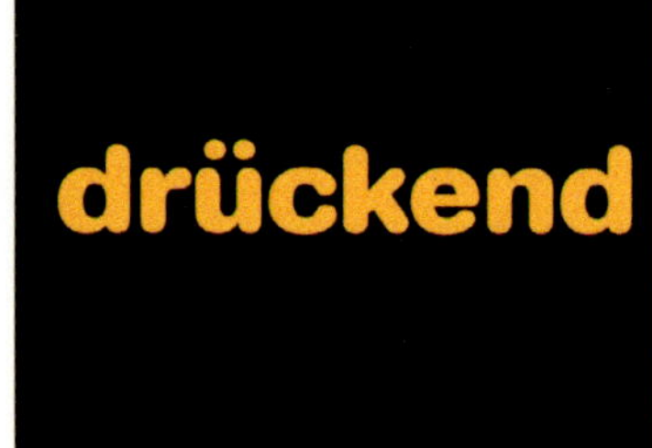

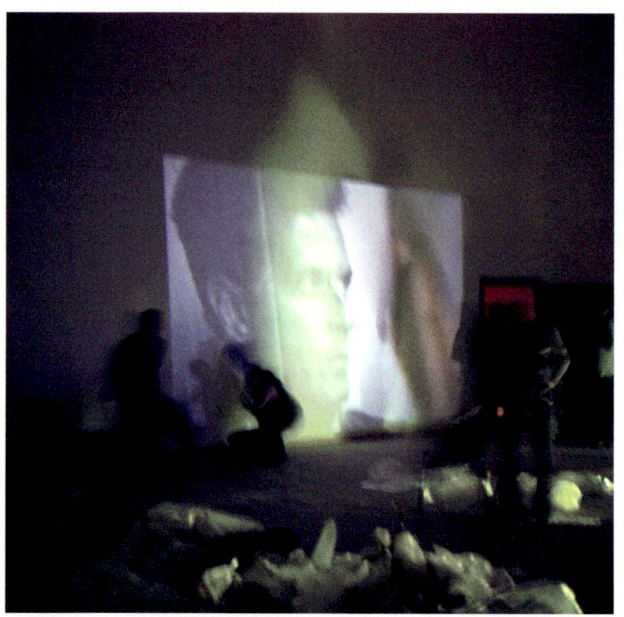

Hogl Pogl, Video 2001

Hogl Pogl, Akademie der
Bildenden Künste München, 2001

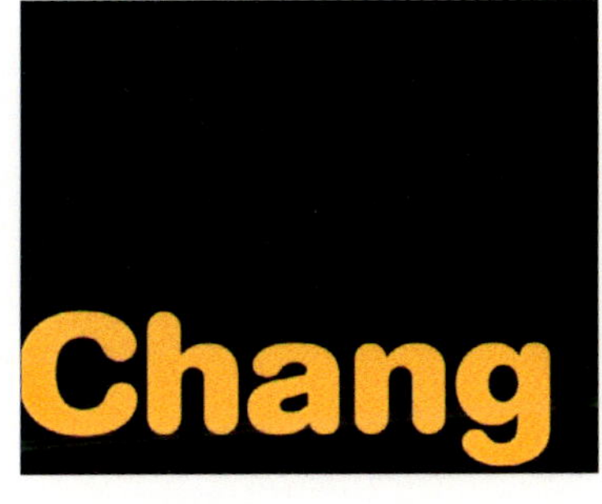
Chang

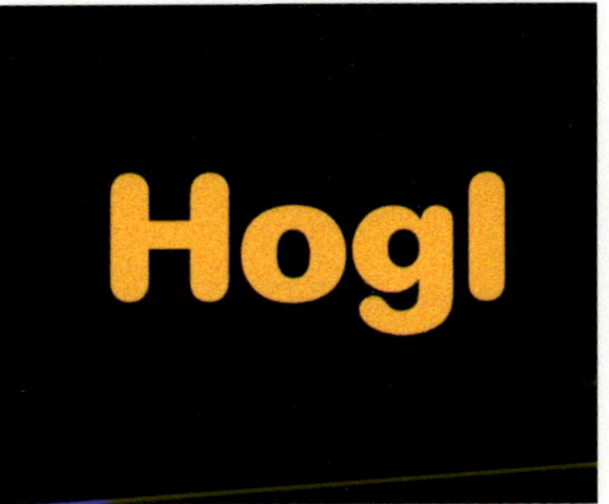
Hogl

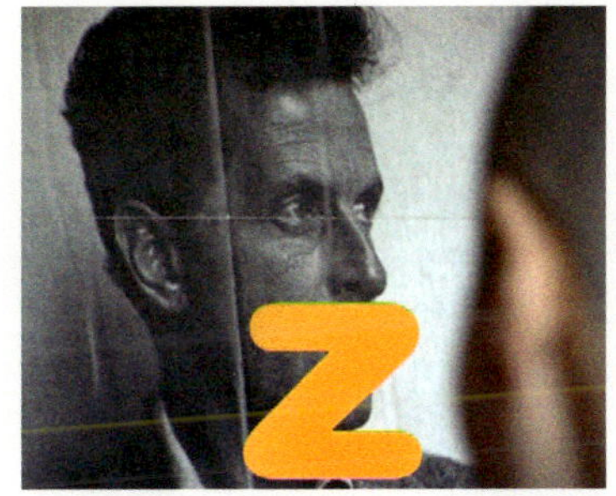
Z

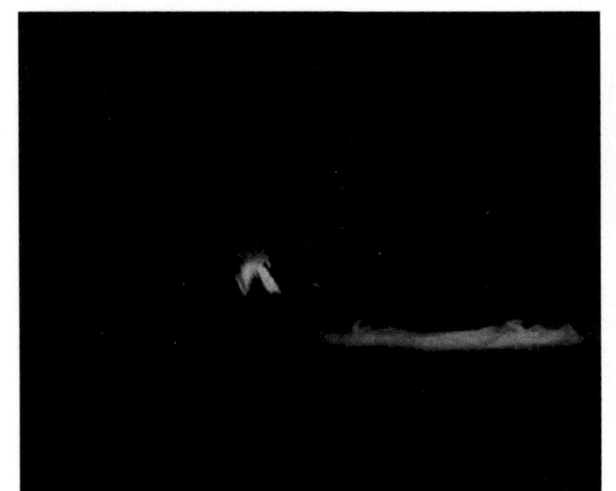
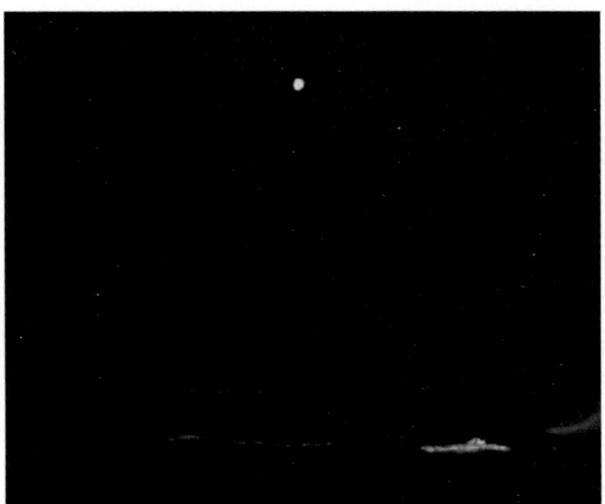
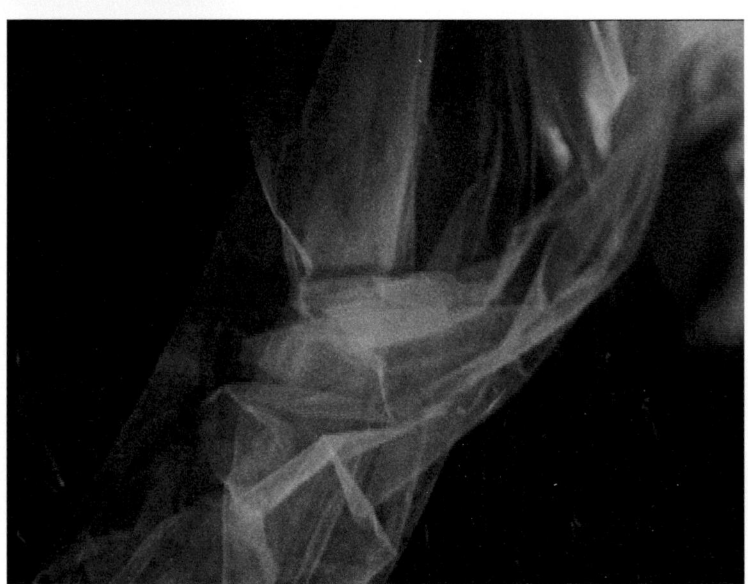

A white raven, Video 2005

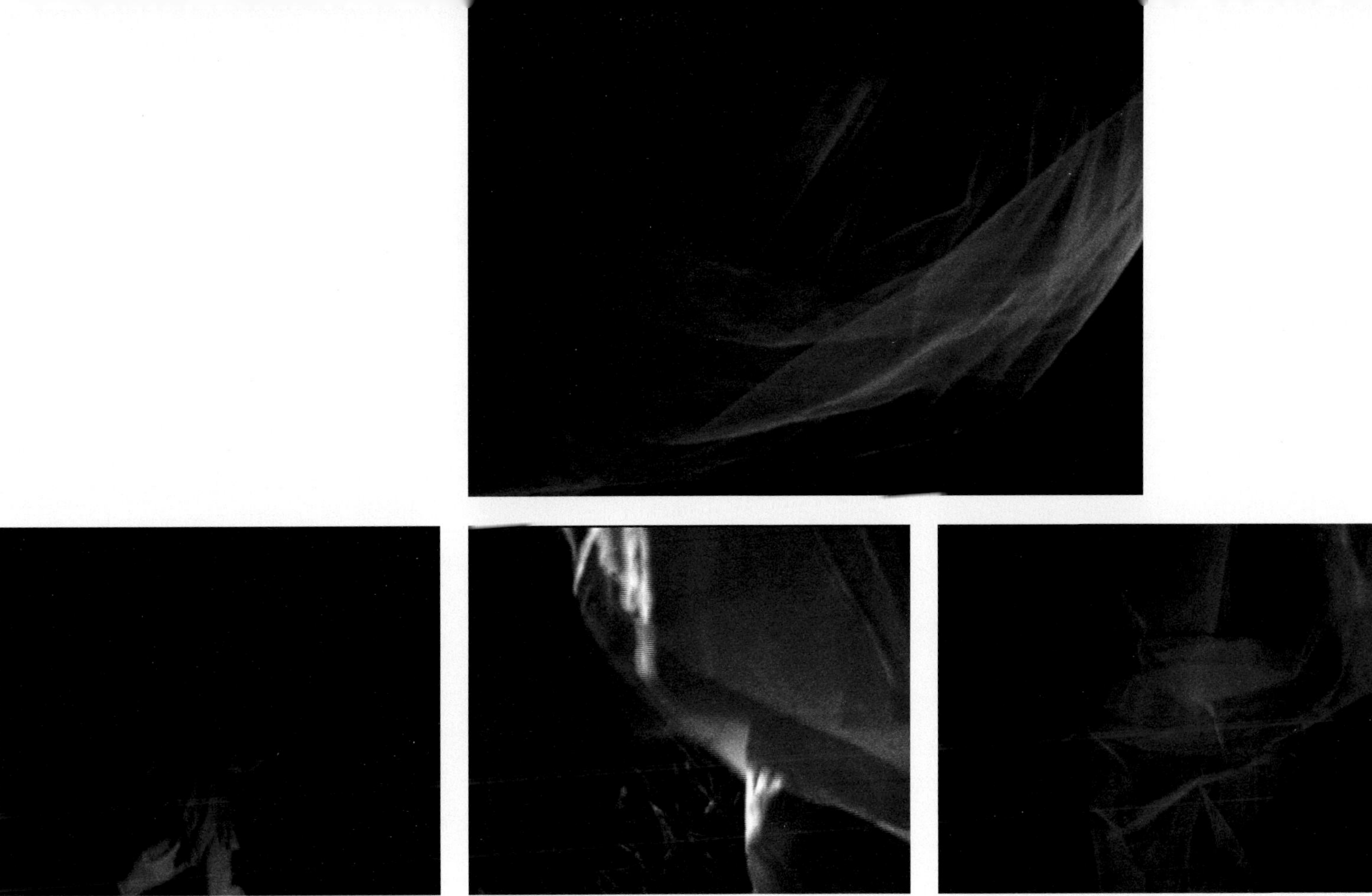

Stephan Huber

»chindalecoht«

Weder von dem Verhältnis des Wortes zum Bild, noch von der Bedeutung subjektiver Gesten oder dem Kontext bestimmter Kleidungsformen, weder weiss ich etwas über regionale Musik, noch über die Bande von Familienbeziehungen. Nun tritt mir aber Snim Ohs Video »chindalecoht« mit der latenten Forderung an dieses kulturelle Wissen gegenüber und legt den Griff ans Telephon nahe, um Bedeutungsebenen nachzufragen. Doch ich bin mir nicht einmal sicher, ob die unterstellte Konnotierung der Arbeit an ihre Biografie überhaupt Vorwissen über fernöstliche Kulturformen erfordert, oder ob ich dem Klischee aufsitze, das Weisse, das Langsame und das Sphärische in ihrer Synthese als typisch »koreanisch zu lesen«.

Ich werde versuchen, diese Videoarbeit aus meinem System heraus zu »lesen«: Ein weisser Raum, weisse Formen, eine weiss gekleidete Person. Lampenschirme, deren Herkunft sicherlich eine fernöstliche ist, heute jedoch über Einrichtungshäuser wie Ikea zum globalisierten Standard gehören, liegen und hängen im Raum. Snim Oh, Protagonistin in ihrem eigenen Film, ist kunstvoll gekleidet: geschichtete und gefaltete Stoffe scheinen auf regionale Kleidung hinzuweisen. Oder ist es doch nur die ästhetische Vorliebe ihrer Extravaganz? Eine Art Performance-Kunstkleidung? Analogien zu James Lee Byars gehen mir durch den Kopf. Doch im Gegensatz zu seinem amerikanischen egozentrischen Ich, scheint Snim Ohs Ich wesentlich stärker in kulturelle Selbsterfahrung eingebunden zu sein. Sie bewegt sich traumwandlerisch lautlos durch den sphärischen Raum und hält die weissen Kugeln in Bewegung. Diese motorische Aktion, zieht sich durch den Film, unterlegt von einem Gesang, von dem ich erahne, dass es Snim Ohs eigene Stimme ist. Das Lied, das mich aufgrund der repetitiven Struktur an gregoranische Gesänge erinnert, trägt eine melancholische Anmutung in sich; aber möglicherweise verheddere ich mich hier im westlichen Gefühlskanon. Ist es ein Kinderlied? Bedeutungsträger in ihrer Biografie? Ich weiss es nicht, aber ich vermute es; auch deshalb, weil ich glaube, dass die eingeblendeten Fotos ebenso mit ihrer Biografie verknüpft sind: entstammen die abgebildeten Personen aus ihrer Familie? Sind es Jugendfotos von ihr selbst? Ist das Video eine Aufarbeitung ihrer Herkunft, eine emotionale Näherung an ihre Familie, die Geschichte ihres eigenen Ichs? Ich vermute es.

Das Video besitzt in seiner Langsamkeit, in seiner weissen Ruhe eine grosse Suggestionskraft. Die langsamen Bewegungen, die ruhigen Überblendungen, der erhabene Kamerastandpunkt und die repetitive Musik verstärken dieses Eingesogenwerden. Die immer ähnlichen Bewegungen – sisyphusartig, jedoch aller Schwere entbunden – scheinen zur Metapher der ständigen Bewegung, des alles-im-Flusses zu werden. Ich ertappe mich, wie ich eine eigene Erzählung zu

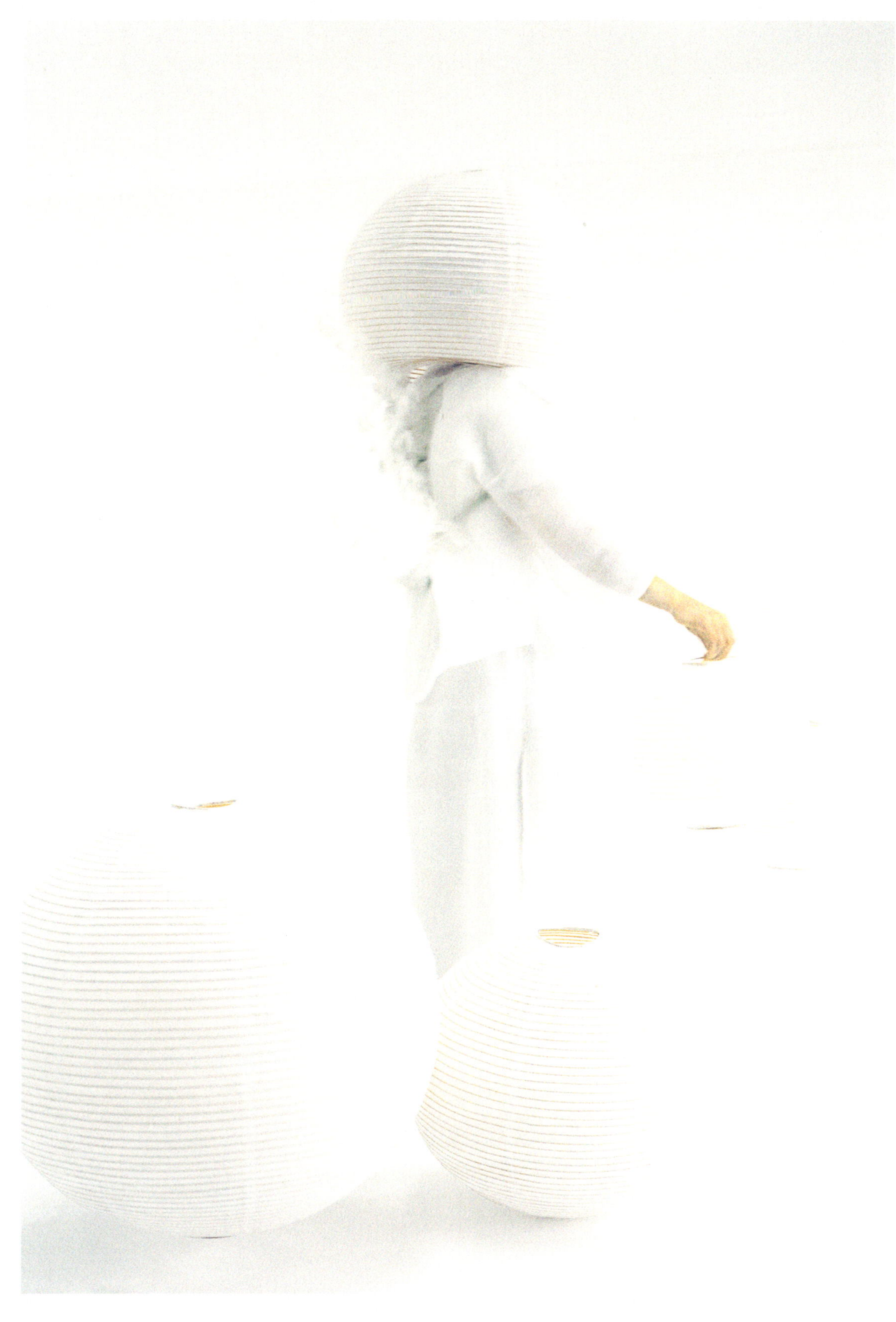

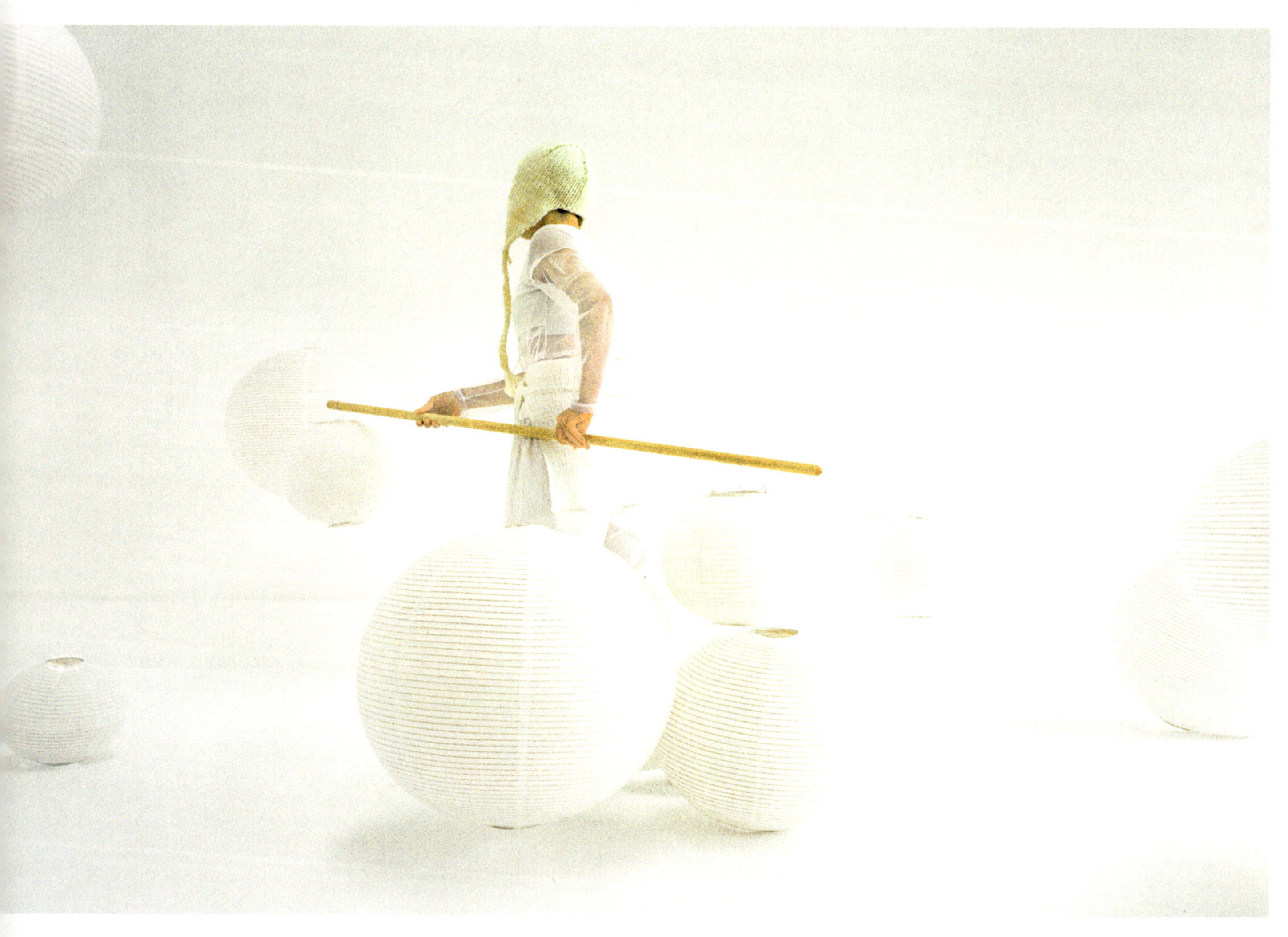

dem Video und den darin verwendeten Fotos aufbaue, die erfüllt ist von zarter Melancholie und ein Gefühl evoziert, alles zu kennen und es dennoch so nie gesehen zu haben.

Die Zeit scheint stillzustehen in diesem Video: es wirkt wie ein Fremdkörper in einer Gattung, deren Ergebnisse hauptsächlich ironisch, bunt/laut/schnell, hybrid und aggressiv geprägt sind. Snim Ohs Arbeit entbehrt jeder Videoclipästhetik oder medialen Schnelligkeit. Es baut ein Geheimnis auf, es ist ein Sinngebilde, das rational nicht dechiffriert wird, sondern über Gefühle den Menschen trifft. Damit steht es – auch wenn es scheinbar aus der Zeit gefallen ist – im Zentrum der Kunst.

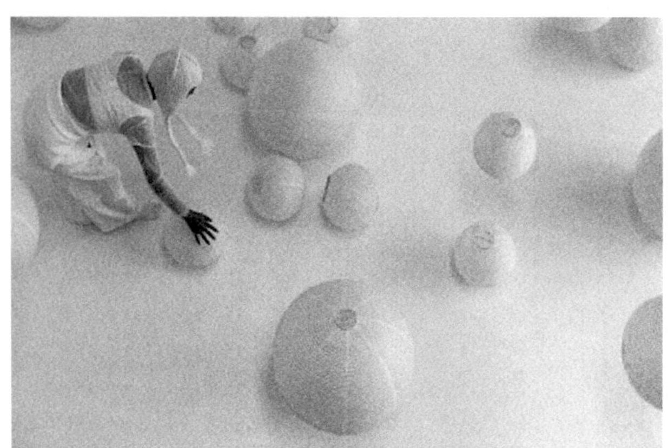

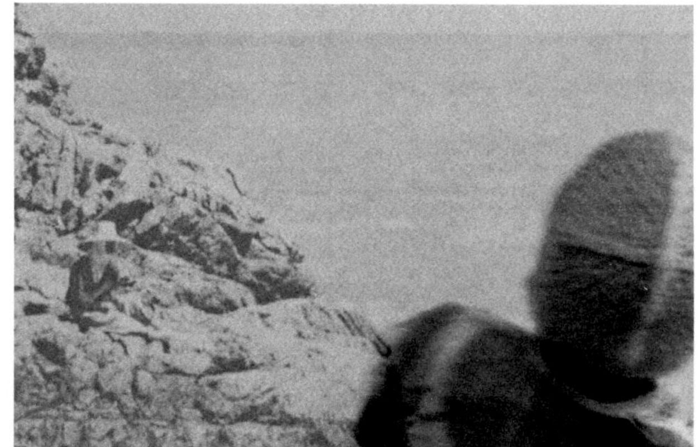

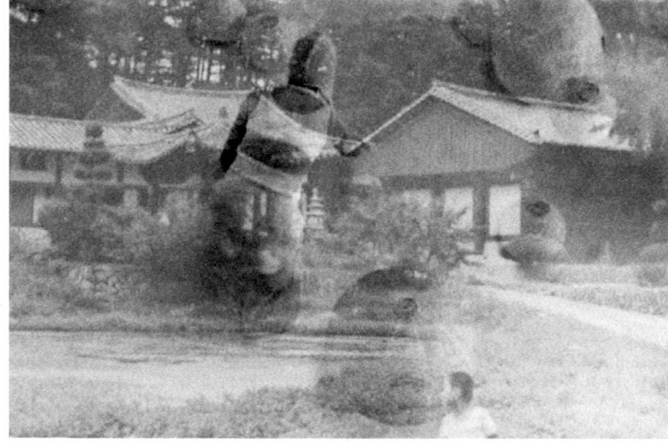

Chindalecoht, Video 2006

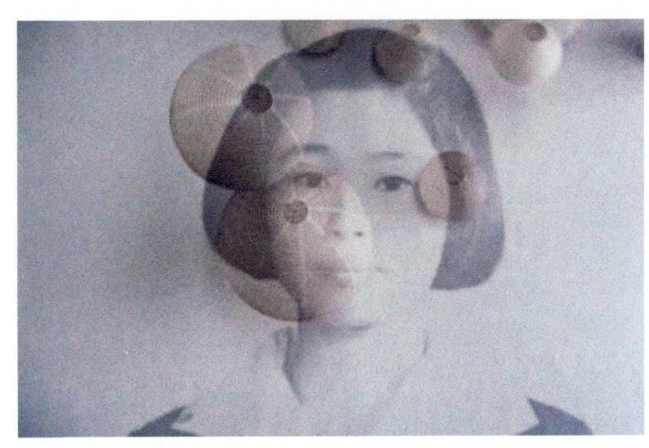

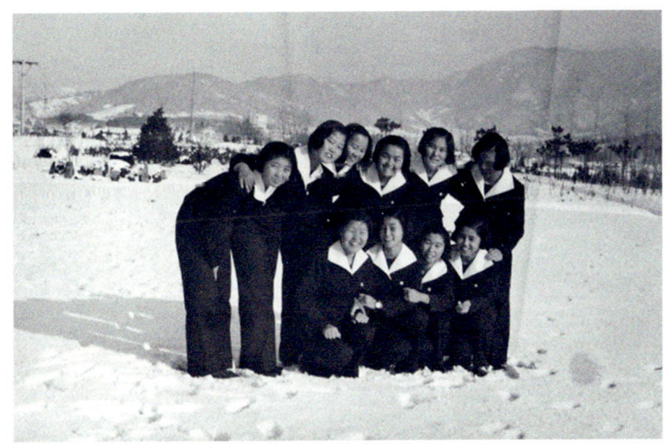

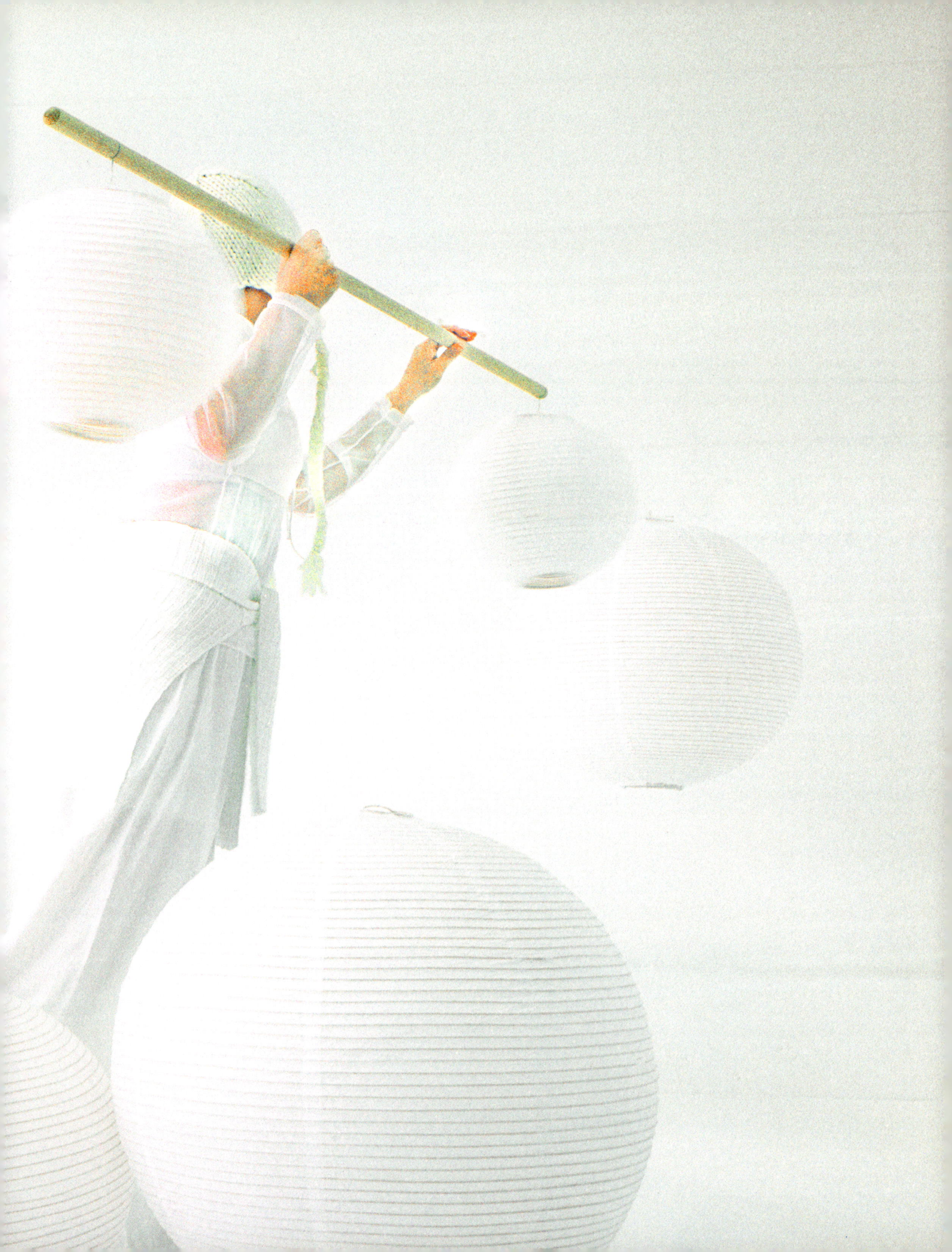

Stephan Huber

»chindalecoht«

About the relationship of the word to the image, the meaning of the subjective gesture, the context of particular forms of clothing, I do not know. Neither do I know anything about the regional music, nor the bonds of family relations.

Now, however, S'nim Oh's video confronts me with a latent demand that I know something about these cultural issues, and it would make sense to pick up the telephone to ask about the levels of meaning. Yet all of a sudden I am not really sure if the supposed connotation of the work through its biography actually requires any previous knowledge of Far Eastern forms of culture, or if I myself am simply appending a cliché to the work by interpreting the synthesis of white, slow, and spherical as »typically Korean«.

I will attempt to »read« this video from the standpoint of my own system: a white space, white shapes, a person dressed in white. Lampshades whose origins must certainly be Far Eastern, but which nowadays have become familiar around the world thanks to stores like Ikea, are lying or hanging in the room. S'nim Oh, the protagonist of her own film, is artfully clothed: layered and folded fabrics seem to be references to regional dress. Or is it just the aesthetic predilection of her extravagance? A kind of performance art costume? Analogies to James Lee Byars go through my mind. Yet in contrast to his egocentric American self, S'nim Oh's self seems to be more strongly bound to the cultural experience of the self. She silently moves like a sleepwalker through the spherical space, keeping a number of white globes in motion. This physical action continues throughout the film, a chanting voice underlying it, and it occurs to me that it could be S'nim Oh's own voice. The song, whose repetitive structure reminds me of Gregorian chanting, has a melancholy beauty, but I'm probably getting muddled up in the canon of western emotions. Is it a children's song? Something from her life that has meaning? I don't know, but I suspect that is the case, also because I believe that the photographs blended in are linked to her biography, too: are the people in the photographs members of her family? Are these pictures of her as a child? Is the video her way of processing her heritage, an emotional approach to her family, the history of her own self? I think so.

In its leisurely pace, its white calm, the video possesses great power of suggestion. The slow movements, the quiet fades, the camera's sublime point of view, and the repetitive music intensify the sense of being drawn into the work. The constant, similar motions – Sisyphus-like, but bereft of all sense of weight – seem to become a metaphor for constant motion, the way that everything eventually becomes one with the flow. I catch myself making up my own narrative about the video and its photographs, which is full of tender melancholy and evokes the sense that all is familiar, although it has never been seen before in this particular form.

Time seems to stand still in this video: it is like a foreign body in a genre whose events are mostly ironic, colorful / loud / fast, hybrid, and aggressive. S'nim Oh's work has absolutely no hallmarks of the video clip aesthetic or the fast pace of most media. It constructs a secret; it is a symbol that is not rationally decoded, but instead affects people through emotion. And thus it stands – even though it appears to have fallen out of time – at the center of art.

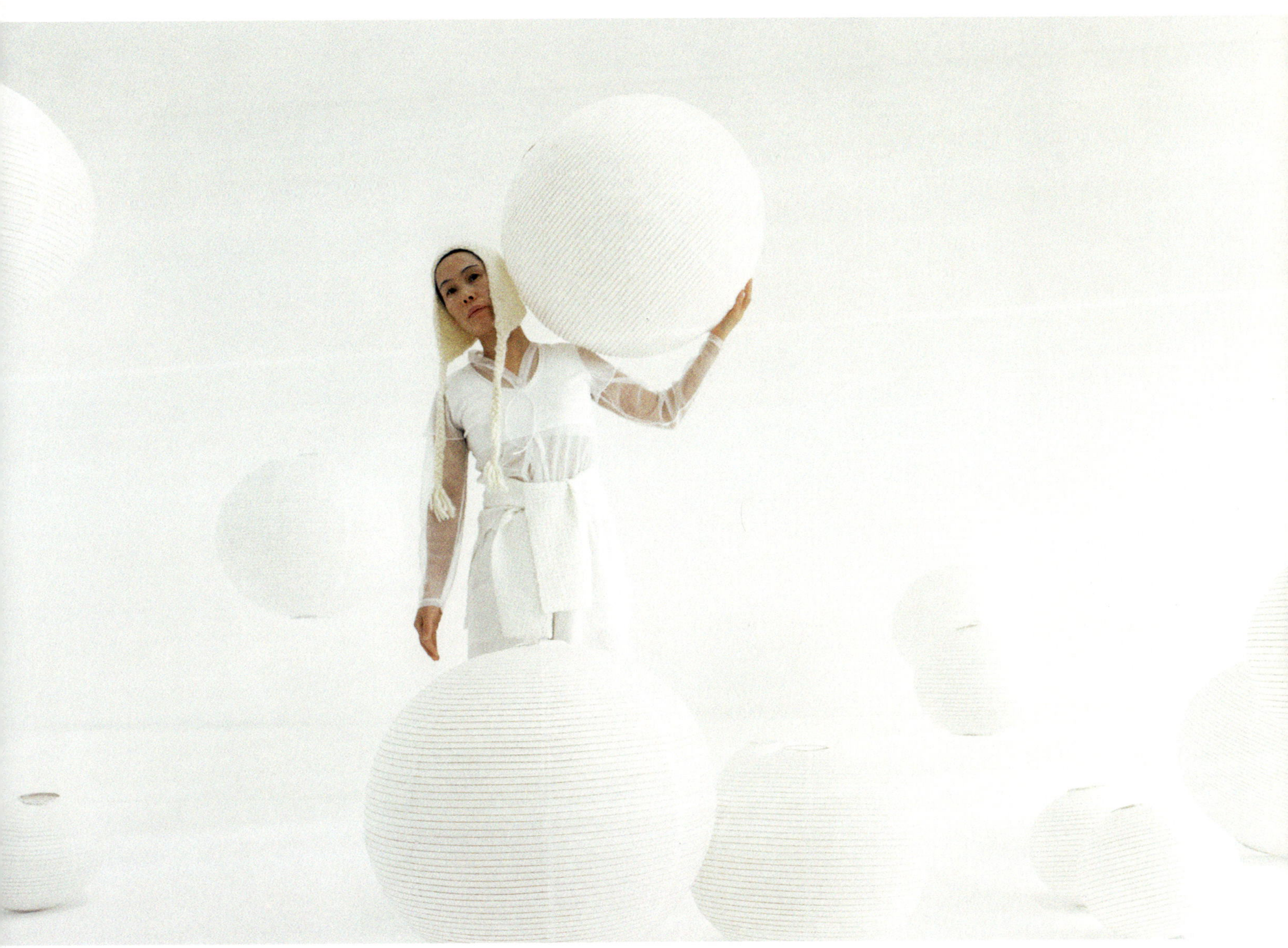

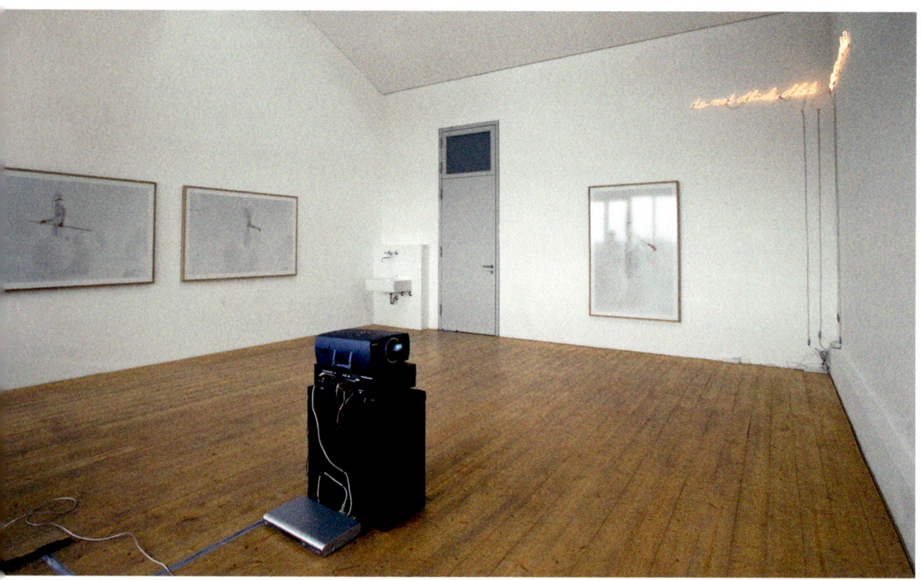

chindalecoht, Akademie der Bildenden Künste, München, 2006

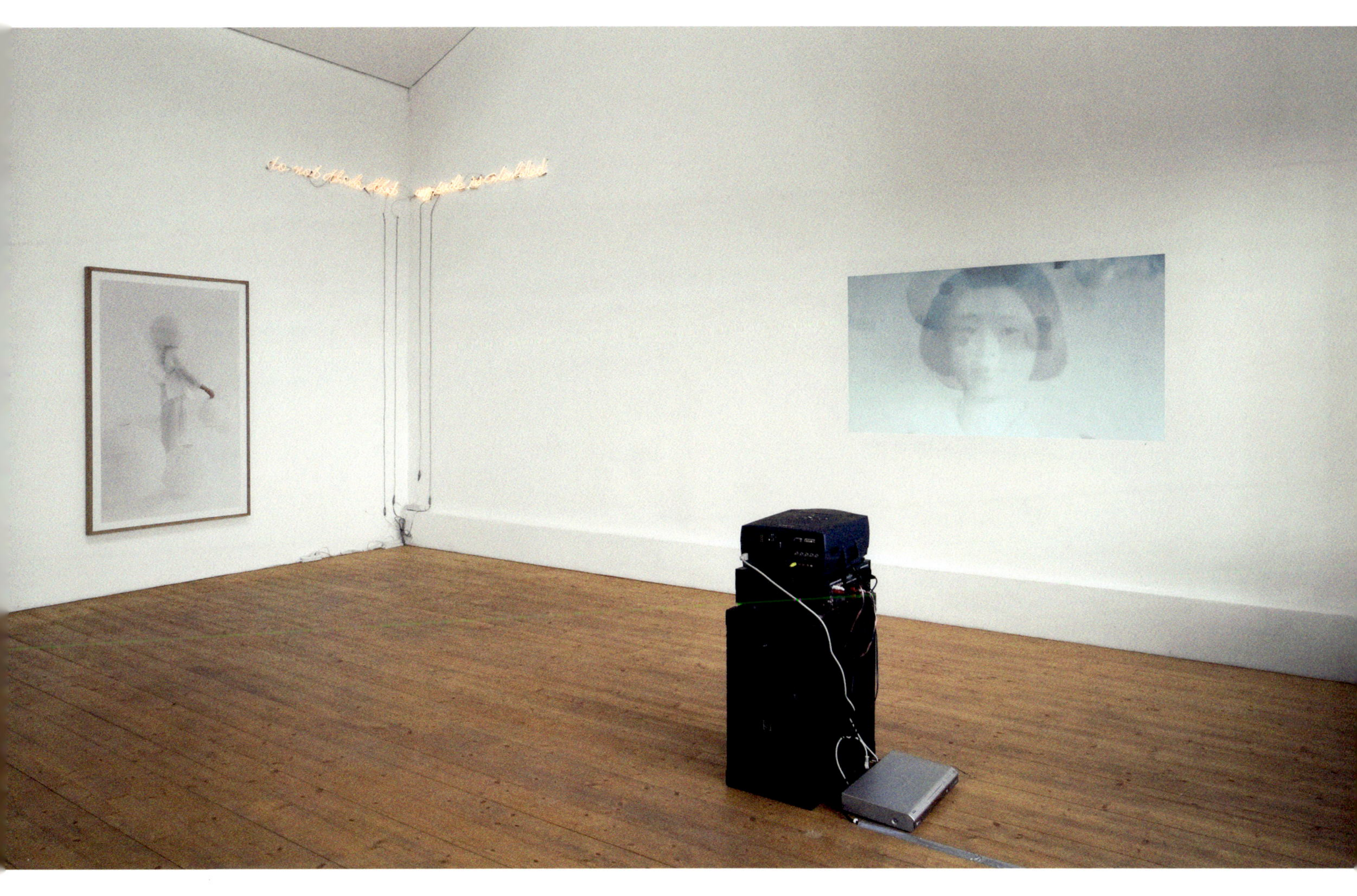

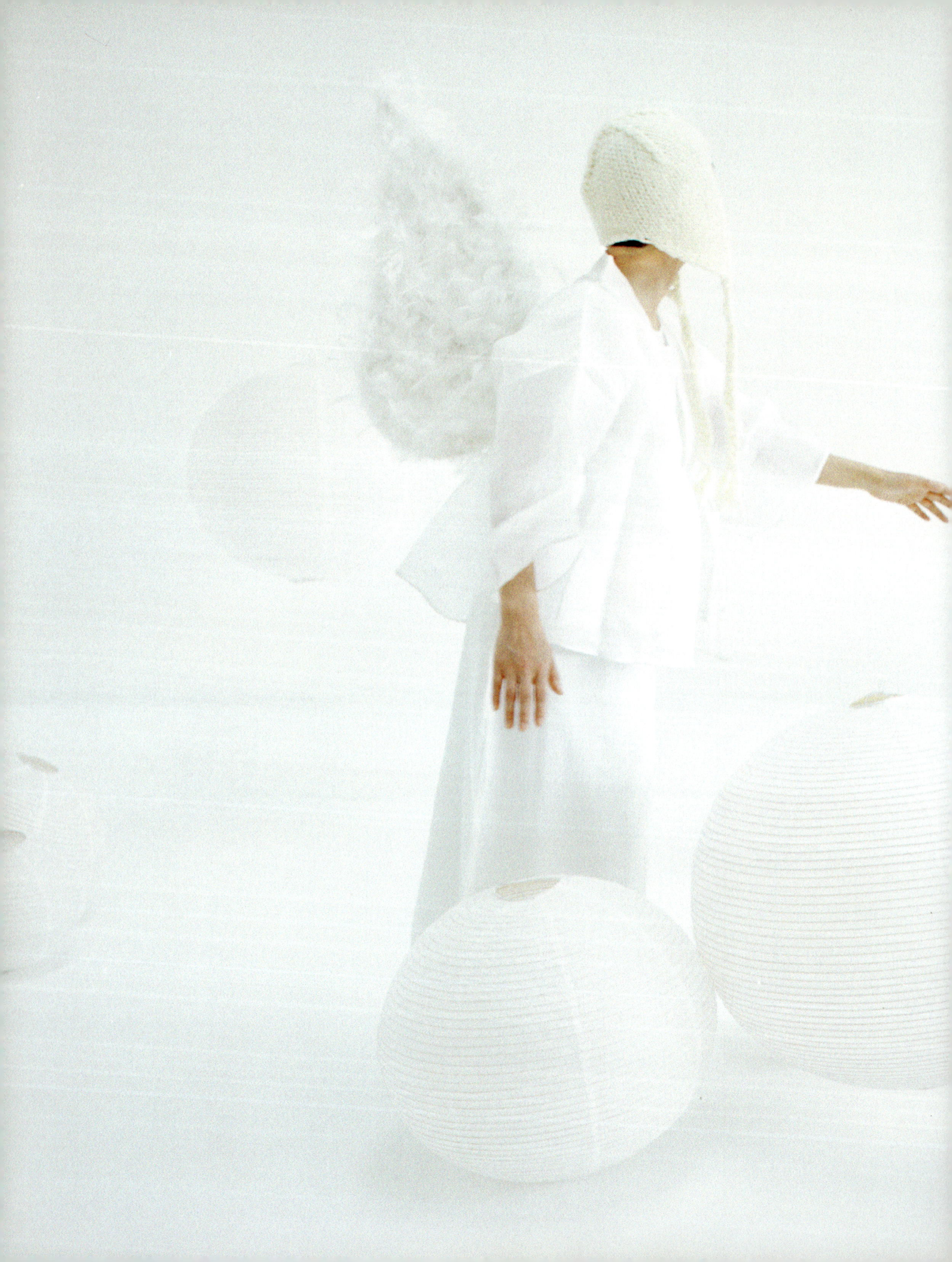

Biographie / Biography

S`nim Oh (south Korea)
lebt und arbeitet in München und Italien/
lives and works in Munich Germany and Italy.

Studium / Education

1999-2005	Akademie der Bildenden Künste München bei Prof. Joseph Kosuth und Prof. Stephan Huber/Academy of Fine Arts in Munich, Germany
1997-2002	Ludwig-Maximilians-Universität (LMU) München, Philosophie / University of Munich, Philosophy PhD.

Stipendien/ Fellowships

2003	Projektstipendium der Erwin und Gisella von Steiner-Stiftung/ Erwin und Gisella von Steiner-Fellowship Munich, Germany
2005	Projektförderung durch die LFA Förderbank Bayern/ LFA Bank-Fellowship Bavaria , Germany Katalogförderungder Erwin und Gisella von Steiner-Stiftung/ Sponsorship for catalog, Erwin und Gisella von Steiner-Fellowship Munich, Germany
2007	Katalogförderung der Autonomen Provinz Bozen, Abteilung für Kultur/ Sponsorship for catalog, provincia Autonoma di Bolzano , department for culture, Italy

Ausstellungen / Exhibitions

2007 Galerie Martin Geier, Meran, Italien/Italy

2006 Diplomausstellung, Akademie der Bildenden Künste München/ Munich, Germany

2005 Galerie der Moderne Stefan Vogdt, München / Munich, Germany

Jahresausstellung Akademie München / Munich, Germany

Weltenburger Spuren, Kloster Weltenburg/Germany

10 Jahre Jubiläum LFA Kunstmesse München / Munich, Germany

Erste Europaische Lithotage München / Munich, Germany

105 km Kreuzherrnsaal Memmingen/Germany
Contemporär Galerie München / Munich, Germany

2004 Akademiegalerie München / Munich, Germany

Jahresausstellung Akademie München / Munich, Germany

2003 Projekt Mahag, Akademie München / Munich, Germany

Stiftung Starke, Berlin / Germany

Jahresausstellung Akademie München / Munich, Germany

PTS München und Baden Baden / Germany

Open Art, Wandergalerie München / Munich, Germany

2002 Galerie im Andechshof, Innsbruck / Austria

Jahresausstellung Akademie München / Munich, Germany

2001 Projekt Münchner Merkur/ Munich, Germany

Kunstbüro Hasenbergl/ Munich, Germany

Video-Projekt
Akademie der Bildenden Künste München/Filmfachhochschule/ Theaterwissenschaft/ LMU-München / Munich, Germany

Werkverzeichnis der abgebildeten Arbeiten/ Index of the works

Seite 6
»Wishes«
C-Print 171 cm x 111 cm, 2005

Seite 10 und 11
»Wishes«
C-Print 171 cm x 111 cm, 2005

Seite 12 und 13
»Wishes«
C-Print 171 cm x 111 cm, 2007

Seite 14 und 15
»Wishes«
C-Print 171 cm x 111 cm, 2005

Seite 16 und 17
Galerie der Moderne Stefan Vogdt
2005

Seite 19
»Wishes«
C-Print 171 cm x 111 cm, 2005

Seite 22 und 23
»Wishes«
C-Print 171 cm x 111 cm, 2005

Seite 24 und 25
White Box, München
2005

Seite 26 und 27
»Wishes«
C-Print 171 cm x 111 cm, 2005

Seite 28 und 29
Contemporär Galerie, München
2005

Seite 30 und 31
»Wishes«
C-Print 171 cm x 111 cm, 2005

Seite 32 und 33
»Wishes«
C-Print 171 cm x 111 cm, 2005

Seite 34 und 35
»Wishes«
Video, 2004

Seite 36 und 37
Jahresausstellung Akademie der Bildenden Künste München
2004

Seite 38 und 39
»Wishes«
Video, 2004

Seite 40 und 41
»Wishes«
Video, 2005

Seite 42 und 43
»Wishes«
C-Print 171 cm x 111 cm, 2005

Seite 44 und 45
»Wishes«
C-Print 171 cm x 111 cm, 2005

Seite 46 bis 53
»Wishes«
C-Print 171 cm x 111 cm, 2006

Seite 57 bis 63
»Schein und Wirklichkeit«
C-Print 171 cm x 111 cm, 2003

Seite 64 und 65
»Schein und Wirklichkeit«
Video, 2003

Seite 69
»Whenever I am in a good mood«
Video, 2003

Seite 70 und 71
»Be aware of your perveted perception«
Video, 2005

Seite 72 und 73
Jahresausstellung Akademie der
Bildenden Künste München
2002

Seite 74 und 75
Galerie im Andechshof Innsbruck
2002

Seite 76 und 77
PTS Kongresssaal Baden Baden
2003

Seite 78 und 79
»Meine Welt ist unaussprechlich«
Video, 2003

Seite 80
Akademiegalerie München
2004

Seite 81
Jahresausstellung Akademie der
Bildenden Künste München
2003

Seite 82 und 83
»Meine Welt ist unaussprechlich«
Stoff und Papier 40 cm x 120cm, 2003

Seite 84 bis 87
»Meine Welt ist unaussprechlich«
C-Print 171 cm x 111 cm, 2003

Seite 88 und 89
»Aspektwechsel«
Video, 2002

Seite 90 und 91
Wandergalerie im Kanzler, München
Open Art, 2003

Seite 92 und 93
»Do not think that my smile is calculated«
Kloster Weltenburg
2005

Seite 94 und 95
»Hogl Pogl«
Video, 2001

Seite 96 und 97
»A white raven«
Video, 2005

Seite 99 bis 103
»Chindalecoht«
C-Print 171 cm x 111 cm, 2006

Seite 104 und 105
»Chindalecoht«
Video, 2006

Seite 106 und 107
»Chindalecoht«
C-Print 171 cm x 111 cm, 2006

Seite 109
»Chindalecoht«
C-Print 171 cm x 111 cm, 2006

Seite 110 und 111
Akademie der Bildenden Künste München
2006

Seite 112 und 113
»Chindalecoht«
C-Print 171 cm x 111 cm, 2006

Impressum

Herausgeber / Editor: Annette Doms
Konzept / Concept: S'nim Oh
Redaktion / Editors: Othmar Prenner, Juliane Handschuh
Texte / Texts: Annette Doms, Daniela Zyman, Stephan Huber

Dr. Annette Doms
Art historian and curator,
2005 to 2007 lecturer of the Academy of Fine Arts in Munich, Germany

Daniela Zyman
Chief curator Thyssen-Bornemisza Art Contemporary in Vienna, Austria

Stephan Huber
Artist and curator, Professor of the Academy of Fine Arts in Munich, Germany

Übersetzung/Translation: Allison Plath-Moseley
Gestaltung / Catalog Design: Juliane Handschuh
Auflage / Edition: 1250

Printed and published by Kerber Verlag Bielefeld
Windelsbleicher Straße 166–170
33659 Bielefeld, Germany
Tel.: +49 (0) 5 21/9 50 08 10
Fax: +49 (0) 5 21/9 50 08 88
E-Mail: info@kerberverlag.com
www.kerberverlag.com

US Distribution
D.A.P., Distributed Art Publishers Inc.
155 Sixth Avenue 2nd Floor
New York, N.Y. 10013.1507
Tel.: 001 212 627 19 99
Fax: 001 212 627 94 84

ISBN 978-3-86678-134-4

Printed in Germany

Sponsored by:

Erwin und Gisela von Steiner-Stiftung / Munich, Germany

Die LFA Förderbank Bayern / Bavaria, Germany

Autonome Provinz Bozen Abteilug für Kultur /
provincia Autonoma di Bolzano, department for culture, Italy

Special thanks to:

Othmar Prenner, Juliane Handschuh, Annette Doms,
LFA Förderbank Bayern, Erwin und Gisela von Steiner-Stiftung,
Autonome Provinz Bozen Abteilug für Kultur